ONE MORE RIDE

ONE MORE RIDE

FRED MILVERSTEDT

August Publications
Middleton, Wisconsin

This book was produced using PressBooks.com, and PDF rendering was done by PrinceXML.

Dedication

To my father for priming the pump, and Fiscus for setting the spark.

Special Thanks:

Mike Baron
Linda McCartney
Joe Schabel
Barbi Wilson Kinney
Marc Eisen
Kevin Reichard

And to everyone who appears in this book. Without you, there would be no story. Not this one, anyway.

Contents

What Others Are Saying About One More Ride

"Reading *One More Ride* is pure pleasure. With an almost magical narrative voice Fred Milverstedt celebrates his lifelong love of bikes and fellow bikers and captures the unique spirit of men and women who feel compelled to do things like rack up 100,000 miles sitting astride an exposed engine and two wheels."
–**David Rhodes**, author of **Jewelweed, The Last Fair Deal Going Down, Driftless**, and **Rock Island Line**

"I greatly enjoyed the book…but hated Fred's riff on guns."
–**David Maraniss**, author of **When Pride Still Mattered: Lombardi** and **Barack Obama: The Story**

"If you've ever had a hankering to get up and get away from it all, Fred Milverstedt's *One More Ride* is the perfect remedy for the winter blues. Follow his adventures and misadventures through America's heartland as he fires up his trusty motorcycle for a modern day Odyssey to Spearfish and Deadwood in what for many enthusiasts has become an annual pilgrimage. Bugs, weather, and mechanical glitches are simply par for the course and how the intrepid pilgrim deals with each is a story unto itself made infinitely better by Fred's subtle humor and unshakable *sangfroid*."
–**Frederick J. Chiaventone**, author of **A Road We Do Not Know: A Novel of Custer at the Little Bighorn** and **Moon of Bitter Cold**

Also by Fred Milverstedt

The Quiet Legend, Henry Aaron

In This Corner, Muhammad Ali

Copyright

August Publications
3543 John Muir Dr.
Middleton, WI 53562
877.343.5207
augustpublications.com

ISBN (print): 978-1-938532-06-1
ISBN (eBook): 978-1-938532-07-8

9 8 7 6 5 4 3 2 1

Editor: Marc Eisen

Cover: Jim Tocco, based on an original concept by Natalie Nowytski

Printed in the United States of America

Introduction

Fred at Van Hise Rock.

While writing this book, I've had occasion to consider what the title might be.

Harrowing Times came to mind, as did *Whew—That Was Close*, m'lady Barbi's favorite, and *Didn't You See That Deer?,* a line my pal Moonie likes to drop on me.

Indeed, there seems to be a preponderance of stories here that, but for the good grace of God and that long streak of luck that so often has favored me, might well have ended in tragedy.

'Course, were that the case, I wouldn't be writing them, would I?

Riding motorcycles, like any other dynamic activity, can be fraught with peril. By contrast, for every time on a given ride you encounter a difficult, sometimes dangerous situation, there are hundreds of times when the rides are magnificent, almost transcendent, and you return home safely and happy as a bug without so much as even a cop coming your way and checking his radar to see if you might have been speeding.

These rides, blissful as they may be, are not exactly the kind of stuff that makes for a well-paced, exciting and entertaining read. It would be boring. And given the kind of writer I am, and the kind I am not, it would be worse.

What I've tried to do here is simply tell stories. More importantly, stories for the most part, for anyone who rides or has ridden, that hardly are anything far out of the mainstream, stories that in biker circles, sitting around and chewing the fat, would even be considered that unusual.

I see myself as an average rider, and it's my hunch that if you've ridden as long as I have, on average, the same sort of things have happened to you.

That, or reasonable facsimiles.

I've ridden 100,000 miles in my life, a fair piece of that in the past few years, and by the time anybody reads this I'll be 70 years old.

Neither is of particular distinction.

In the world of motorcycling, it takes 100,000 miles to break in your leathers, the time it takes before you really start getting the hang of it. Among bikers who ride, who profess to ride, 100,000 miles is all but obligatory.

What it actually means is quite subtle. It means that you've ridden long or far enough to have "time in the saddle" and it shows. Others know it, too, and you don't have to tell them. There's an aura. It seeps out through the scuff of your boots, the seams and cracks of your chaps, jacket and riding vest. For bikers who ride, it's an intuitive recognition—this guy's been around.

The older the better.

An adage: There are bold bikers and there are old bikers, but there are few bold and old bikers.

There's a fella round here they call Wild Bill who buys a new bike every couple of years and rides them on the average of 75,000 miles annually.

Wild Bill is well into his 80's.

Tough old cuss, wise, and still going strong.

Makes me feel like a whippersnapper.

Best I could do alongside Bill is see if I could hold my own, try to keep up.

I'm not in Bill's class, but I'm seasoned, and so are many of you. In the stories here, I believe, you'll find pretty much the same stories you've lived yourselves—the general drift, anyway.

In the realm of motorcycles, much has already been written, and together they comprise a genre.

This is my contribution.

One More Ride.

1

RIDE THE WILD WIND

Southwestern Wisconsin

1994

2

Prairie Dog Town

It was the highway patrolman who tipped us off to the state of our peril.

It must have been midnight or so, in a truck stop in Mauston. A cop parks his cruiser out front, gives the bike the once-over, walks in and sits down in the booth behind us. It's me and Mar, having a coffee.

"You must have been blowing around pretty good out there," sez he.

"Yeah, we hit some pretty good gusts," I allow.

"Well, for what it's worth, I just had one blow me across two lanes of highway."

Gulp.

Turns out the worst of our suspicions was confirmed. A storm front had started moving across Iowa and southern Minnesota early in the afternoon, and by 4 p.m. the first inklings of it were ominously apparent as we cruised the high ridges and narrow winding roads deep in the valley of the Kickapoo River, about 30 miles inland from the Mississippi and about halfway between La Crosse and Prairie du Chien.

We'd seen the clouds gathering to the northwest, then heard about what we were in for from a guy on a Buell who pulled in behind us to gas up in the little hamlet of Gays Mills, apple-orchard capital of southwest Wisconsin. The Buell was missing a few parts, he said, but you couldn't prove it by us. It looked plenty fast and mean. He was heading home, he said, trying to beat the storm. He told me about a shortcut I could take from State 131 over to State 27, which would take me back down the west side of the valley into Prairie du Chien, saving about 20 miles.

We were riding the Shadow 750, the fourth of my Hondas, and were coming in by way of a meandering 160-mile route with our primary destination the Fur Traders Rendezvous on the grounds of old Fort Crawford in Prairie du Chien: the "Prairie of the Dog" or better yet, "Prairie Dog Town," as a good pal, Bugsy, used to call it. The rendezvous was one in a series of summer encampments of a group of re-enactors who are hard into history, period 1820-1850, when everything west of the Ohio River was still purty much Indian Country, vast, wild and adventurous.

The re-enactors emulate this life, traveling throughout the summer from camp to camp, living in villages of tents and teepees and lean-tos with their wives and kids. When the rubes come around to gawk, they sell them leathers and axes and pelts, beads and jewelry with a fair sense of authenticity—that is, if you can keep from noticing that an unusually large number of the trappers and traders are portly middle-aged white men, long hair and beards with enormous bellies hanging out over their breach-cloths. Indians are scarce.

By 5 p.m. we were seated at the bar of Denny's Sawmill Saloon on Blackhawk Avenue in Prairie Dog Town. The crowd had started shuffling in from the rendezvous, which the sheriff had just closed down, scant blocks away at the river. The wind was picking up, the sky was darkening, and at the Sawmill you could see splatters of rain on the front window through the neon beer signs. On the TV, in and around putts and tee shots at the U.S. Open, the weather service was tracking the storm, showing which counties were in for severe weather, which had tornado-type winds.

There was kidding about it at the Sawmill, with folks asking Denny if he was selling tickets to the basement, which, we soon learned, was not just a joke because two days before they'd had a twister touch down, and people all over town were ducking into basements, vault coolers and bathtubs to ride out the blow. We'd seen the damage, lots of it, all the way from Richland Center.

For our part, we had a motel room booked in La Crosse. That's 60 miles to the north, up the eastern bank of the Mississippi on U.S. 35, what they call the Great River Road. Thanks to the grandeur of the setting, it's some of the best two-lane highway in America, a nice combination of curves and intermingling straights, woods and towering bluffs on the Wisconsin side, and across the river, the bluffs of Iowa and Minnesota. From just northeast of Dubuque, Iowa, it runs a little more than 250 miles to Superior, Wisconsin. From Prairie Dog Town to La Crosse, it's a little less than halfway. Our intention had been to hit the rendezvous, then head up to La Crosse in early evening with the sun setting over the bluffs, and overnight there.

Now, however, we were stuck in a bar, and the fates were about to have their way with us.

The storm appeared to be breaking, at least where we were, so around 8 p.m. we decided to make a run for it. The fates were waiting. We were out on the road barely three miles when the rain started again. For the next two hours, on a trip that normally would take little more than half that, we rode through pelting rain and thunder and lightning at about 45 mph, the only bike on the road.

The skies to the north were as threatening as I'd ever seen, a dark purple. Traffic was comparatively light (thankee, Lord, for that), but most of it was coming our way, cars and trucks, headlights hitting the beads on my windscreen and making visibility difficult, a mild way of putting it.

In the flash of a bolt, reflecting the froth of Old Muddy, I was reminded of two things I don't like about riding, especially at night: lightning storms and visibility. We weren't wearing helmets, so the rain was stinging my face, beads streaming down—on the windscreen, glistening in the headlights. I couldn't see through it.

We did have our rain gear—which, I must say, kept us perfectly warm and dry, at least from our necks down to our ankles. That kept us from getting sopped. But if you've ever been out in a good lightning storm, try it sometime while you're caught between dark, towering bluffs on one side and the Mississippi River on the other. Two wheels and an engine, and the mercy of God.

Or Odin.

Or the Great Thunderbird.

Quite a rush.

I was wearing goggles over my glasses, with the hood of the rain jacket pulled up over a leather baseball cap. That kept most of the rain from blinding me, but with the windshield all but worthless, I had to stick my head out to the left, peering around it whenever there were cars in my face, which was all too often. It got so bad that somewhere just south of Victory, we pulled off the road.

This spot in the state is of interest to me because of its place in regional American Indian lore. In 1832, it was the site of a battle that ended the Black Hawk War.

As chief of the Sac and Fox, Black Hawk and his tribes had been rousted from northern Illinois and a corner of Iowa by the U.S. Army and militia. In a series of classic guerrilla fights, they held off the troops on a strategic retreat across southern Wisconsin, even turning them back on a prairie north of the Wisconsin River called Wisconsin Heights. At the Mississippi, however, the Indians ran out of turf. The Army had a gunboat on the river, the troops closed in and an estimated 400-500 Sac and Fox were killed. For a hundred or so who sought to escape across the Mississippi, their rivals the Sioux were waiting. They took many scalps.

It was the Battle of Bad Axe, and to commemorate it, there's a small historical marker on the east side of the highway as you come upon

Victory. Some historians today call it a massacre. As far as these things go, given interpretations, I'm inclined to agree.

On this night in Victory, there was little to celebrate. We stopped off at a sparse little motel that I ridden past scores of times, hoping for a bit to duck out of the rain. All was dark. They'd lost their power, so for us it was only a temporty respite over a cold cup of coffee, generously offered. My leather gloves were soaked, so I wrung them out.

We finally made it to La Crosse, then started looking for the motel. Naturally, Murphy's Law at work, it was not where the *dummkopf* who gave us directions said it would be. Around 10:30, after circling the north side of the city near the foot of Grandad Bluff, we finally got a tip to the right from a checkout girl who was closing down a Stop 'n' Rob at a strip mall. We pulled up to the office to find nobody there. There was a message on the door, instructing late arriving guests to call a number, which we did, only then to be told—and here's where it really gets good—that neither our credit card nor our phone number had checked out after we phoned in our reservation the day before. They wrote us off, renting the room to somebody else.

While neither Mar nor I were ever ranked by Forbes for our credit rating or wealth, we thought we had this one covered. Nope. T.S., kids.

Now, granted, it's only 11 o'clock—on a Saturday night, yet. But this is La Crosse, Wisconsin, population on the average of 50,000, and because college is not in session and there were no festivals in Riverside Park that runs alongside the river, there was barely anyone to be seen. It was raining, sure, but to find inhabitants I'd have to start trolling the bars along Third Street or possibly dragging the river. There are lots of bars in La Crosse, same as most of Wisconsin. You may have heard.

Still, you'd think you could find one lousy room. Only later did we learn there was a cycle convention in the area that weekend. A big one. Bicyclists from all over had converged, rented all the rooms, and for the weekend were riding the Elroy-Sparta State Trail, 32 miles following old railway corridors and dropping from I-90 down into the Kickapoo Valley in the heart of Wisconsin's non-glaciated region.

At this point then, we really had only two choices. I should have taken the first, which would have been to head back down the river 60 miles into the teeth of the storm and call upon the good graces of friends we knew who lived just outside of Prairie du Chien. But no, not greatly enamored of the teeth of the storm, I went for the second.

"Screw it," I said. "Let's go to Madison."

3

Deer Alley

Slouching out of La Crosse, we commenced the next leg of what now had become a harrowing trail—down 106 miles of interstate through six counties lashed by windstorms and rain, making a grand total of nine counties covered since we'd left Madison at 11 a.m., all of them under tornado watch or severe storm warnings sometime during the day.

On top of this, we'd be traveling through one of the highest concentration of deer in the state, a large and active chunk of a 1.4 million herd. "Deer Alley," I call it. To the buggers' credit, we saw only two—one lying dead on the median grass, a fresh kill judging from the bright red blood on the highway, and a live one who stood there in the trees to our right and watched us coolly as we motored by.

I hate riding I-90 and I-94 in Wisconsin, even under ideal weather conditions, because of the goddamn deer. I always end up feeling like a fighter pilot, one eye on the road, the other peeled tensely for bandits and Zekes.

You might wonder why we weren't wearing helmets.

First, there is the matter of peripheral vision, or the lack of it as I saw it back then. A reduction in the ability to hear what may be coming up beside you is another. But mostly, in the early '90s when this particular odyssey took place, I was still ground into the old school; that is, helmets just weren't very cool. Today I have a different perspective, albeit not much, and am usually glad to at least to have one on board in the event of inclement weather or cold. On extended "slab runs," long cruises on interstates, I tend now to put it on.

But at this juncture in my return to riding, I still wasn't sold on them. Foolish me. We could both have used the cover. Instead, bowing to the elements, I opted for the only option available. I switched my baseball cap around and pulled the peak down tight over my forehead. And I took off both eyeglasses and goggles so there were two less screens between my eyes and the road to have to try and wipe off.

My eyesight, which until early in my 40's was 20/10, "better than perfect," had gone to hell in a handbasket. I could see the road signs ahead, but until passing by was unable to read them. In this case it didn't matter all that much—we both were acutely aware that Madison was straight down 90/94, with any kind of luck somewhere between us and Milwaukee.

On I-90, some 20 to 30 miles east of La Crosse, we pulled off the interstate briefly at a state patrol station that was just closing. The trooper gave us a nearly sympathetic look and said we could hang around under the eaves, should we like. Back on the road, still looking for a room in motels at the first three towns that we passed, no luck, no vacancies. It was the goddamn bicyclists.

One a.m. found us at the truck stop in Mauston, the highway patrolman cluing us in.

"Across two lanes of highway," he sez—in his cruiser—and he let us listen to his radio to underline the point.

Wind gusts of 60 mph, indeed.

The cop, we learned, had ridden bikes much of his life. Until around '85, it mostly was Harleys, he said, and having "probably ridden a half-million miles," he finally got sick of repairing them. "Wouldn't own one today," he said, and commenced to rattle off a list of characteristics that would not go over well at the Motor Company, not in the least "the vibrations that leave your hands numb after 50 or 60 miles." A

Gold Wing, he said, was the best bike he'd owned, the kind he had now.

He looked out at the Shadow. "That's not a very big bike."

He was right. Wringing wet, which it was, the weight went around 465 pounds. Add us, wringing wet, for another 250. For long highway riding, that's not very much. For turbulent winds, you're insane.

He didn't flat out tell us we were crazy, but I think he knew that we knew, and unless we wanted to sit there drinking coffee and eating cherry pie for the next six, seven hours, we didn't really have much of a choice. Oh, I suppose we could have bought magazines, a couple boxes of doughnuts, even dozed in the booth. But by that time, I had my teef into it.

Actually, back at Camp Douglas a few miles to the west, sitting in the lot of another motel, this one six units, I had suggested to Mar that we just leave the bike for a couple of hours and crawl in under the branches of this pine tree that grew between the motel and a gas station. With our leathers on, rain gear over that, plus a soft bed of needles and nature's canopy, I figured, we could have copped a decent snooze, which at that point we were beginning to desperately need. I was getting foggy, my wrists, right arm and lower back aching, and I had a cramp in my right leg. Mar, coming upon the arthritic and recently recovered from a surgically repaired shoulder and neck, was just as exhausted.

"I'm not going in there," sez she, nodding to the tree.

"Why not?" I asked

"Because of Lyme disease."

"Lyme disease!" I said. "I'm worried about getting blown off the interstate and into the horns of an eight-point buck and you're worried about Lyme disease?

"Look, you're wearing all that stuff. The worse thing that could happen is that a tick would crawl into your ear."

Preparing to leave, I put analgesic pain cream on my wrists and we each popped an 800-mg Ibuprofen, resignedly resuming our route.

Still 85 miles from Madison, we damn near made it home without further incident. But some 10 miles northwest of the city, along came the worst gust of the trip. It hit hard and sudden, started to blow us off to our left into the passing lane, then switched directions and drove us back toward the shoulder, basically picking up and shaking us the way a terrier does to a rat. I was lying flat on the tank, Mar hanging over my back.

"Don't you think it's time we get off?" she consulted, hollering into my ear.

Yep, yep, lil' lady—no argument from me.

So we copped a break. We were within several hundred feet of the next exit, Sun Prairie and Waunakee, Madison suburbs connected by County 19. We waited out the worst of the following winds on the leeward side of a truck stop, then crept along 19 a few miles, took the old airport road and sneaked carefully the last few miles into town. I thought we were in.

But no, the fates had one more cruel trick to play.

At the intersection of Johnson and East Washington Avenue, a four-lane boulevard, the street was flooded. It was deep, up to my foot pegs, and I started to rooster tail, then fishtail. To keep it afloat, hoping it wouldn't conk out, I geared down into first and basically frog-marched it the next six blocks to Winnebago, our turn-off, and another six up Willy Street where we sloshed another block and a half to Jenifer Street and our flat. We parked in the driveway, sat there a minute, sighed deeply as one, and walked up the front steps and through our front door.

Exhausted, Mar went to bed right away. I popped open a beer, the first of several, and rolled a number. I sat on the living-room couch, watching a semblance of dawn appear through the haze and the rain, and mused rhetorically, “What have we just come through?”

I promised myself I’d never do it again—leastwise not without a portable tent that I could pitch at a wayside, which would at least keep us off the road and reasonably dry until the rain halted. ‘Course, in those winds, I’m not sure I could ever have got it up, and if I did, chances are the winds would have swept us up and blown us all the way to Lake Michigan.

It was 7 a.m. when Mar got up and found me still sitting there.

“I don’t think I’ve ever loved you so much,” she said.

“Thanks,” I said. “Me, neither.”

4

COWBOY UP

Madison and Environs

1966-1971

Moonie, Fred, and Barbi at the Van Hise Rock, in the Driftless Area.

5

A Groovy Little Motorbike

My father rode bikes in the 1920s, then off and on through the next 40 years. During college, he once rode to Middleton, six miles away, with three others on board. It was winter, he said.

I tried that, pulling out of the parking lot of Jingles Stadium Bar in Madison one night. There were three of us, Apple, riding tail-gun, and a pal named Landy, scrunched in between. I made it out into the street, began to turn left, but when Apple started wriggling around, over we went. Apple and Landy stepped off, but I went down to my left, the bike lying over my leg and pinning me to the concrete.

The gash to my knee was minor, but it became infected, and I was laid up for the better part of a month. Being the spring, it was nearing semester exams. I didn't make any, didn't bother to call and explain, and in the process flunked out of college. The sophomore slump in my junior year.

Some 20 years previous, my father's last real motorcycle was an Indian, a model equipped with what was then popularly known as a "suicide shift," a clutch stick mounted next to the tank rather than a lever on the handlebar. He'd sold it by the time I was a tot, but then in the late '40s when I was only three or four, he bought a Cushman scooter.

He once laid down a tarp on the living-room floor of our small apartment on Langdon Street, rode the scooter up three broad steps, down the hall and through our front door, and took it apart. My mother was not amused. He'd take me for rides, Little Fritzie standing up between his legs on the step-through board, buzzing out Johnson Street at 30 miles per hour, and again mom disapproved.

"You didn't take him on the motorcycle again, did you?" she'd ask.

Naah—of course not.

Curiously, however, when I came of age, it was my father who didn't want me to have one. It wasn't because of the danger or risk; he said it makes a "loner" of you.

I didn't get one until the summer of '65, two years after I got out of the Navy. I was going to college and though still living at home, I guess the old man figured I was old enough to know what I wanted, if not that I knew what I was doing.

It wasn't much of a bike. It really was a scooter, but done up in a nifty little package that made it look almost like a real motorcycle—a Honda S90, a slightly upgraded version of the 50cc step-through scooters with which Honda had introduced itself to the American market a year or two before, their first entry into a field largely dominated hitherto stateside by Harley-Davidson, BMW, the British Triumphs, BSAs and Royal Enfields. It was the S90's looks that caught my fancy, that and a popular song at the time, "Little Honda" by the Beach Boys.

It's not a big motorcycle
Just a groovy little motorbike
It's more fun than a barrel of monkeys
That two-wheel bike
We'll ride on out of the town
To any place I know you like

First gear, it's alright
Second gear, I lean right
Third gear, hang on tight
Faster, it's alright

The Beach Boys were big at the time, wedging a place in my own musical lexicon, which ranged from Benny Goodman to Cozy Cole, Frankie Lane and Johnny Ray, to Hank Williams, Elvis, Chuck Berry, Jerry Lee Lewis and the Everly Brothers. The Beatles had only recently debuted, and I preferred the Stones.

Yet another motivator was the Honda's diminutive size—90 cc's worth of engine, a 47-inch wheel base, a little more than six feet in total length, and a weight of less than 200 pounds—small enough that at 5'7" and 130, something I figured I could handle.

The first one I saw on the street belonged to a guy I had known in high school. Mike Fiscus was his name and I'd seen him tooling around town, the west side of Madison, and admired both his mount and his style, a sort of Dead End Kid Meets James Dean. "You ought to get one," he said. "It's a blast."

A couple of days later I hitched a ride out to the Honda dealer at the Westgate Shopping Center. They had one on the floor—an S90, black tank with a chrome panel insert and gun-metal gray fenders, sitting there on its center stand. I paid $400 and then asked him how it works.

Briefly, he ran me through the basics: Here's the throttle, front brake and clutch levers, rear brake and shift pedal, which in the S90's case, unlike most motorcycles made then or now, was a heel-and-toe apparatus that made it easier to go up and down from gear to gear without having to slip the front of your left foot beneath the shift peg and toe it up.

"Do you know how to drive a stick?" the salesman asked. "It's pretty much the same thing."

So off I went, astride on the flats of my feet, walking it through the back door and out to the parking lot. I got it started, it stalled, then after a few coughs and fits, slipped it into gear and puttered my way up the road.

The plan was that I would rendezvous with Fiscus. I did, following him around for an hour or two on west side city streets, and then he asked if I was "ready for the Arboretum."

The Arboretum, owned by the University of Wisconsin, is comprised of some 1,200 acres of restored prairie, woodlands and wetlands at the edge of Lake Wingra, which at the time comprised the southern side of the city. For motorists, bikers, bicyclists, runners and strollers, it was loved for its three miles of narrow, twisty, paved roadway. In the 1960's, before it became blocked to motorized traffic, it also delighted the stupid and adventuresome, especially those with a heavy hand or foot on the throttle.

Fiscus, knowing I was a novice, set a leisurely pace, maybe 35 miles per hour. I trailed, some three or four bike lengths behind. The first two sweeping turns I navigated successfully. It was at the third and fourth, a downhill right and then a reverse camber left, when I had the brief but highly visceral sensation that I ought to be leaning more.

Leaning on a bike, so critical to riding, is something I had yet to learn. I drifted into the shoulder, rode it down until the left-foot peg dug into the gravel and sand, and with that abrupt and jarring halt of motion, flew over the handlebars and off into the high-side thicket.

Fiscus, out of sight and well around the next couple of turns, glanced into a mirror and noticed I was missing. He turned around, came back up the road and arrived just time to see me emerge from the brush, scratched, dusty and picking at twigs, but amazingly without anything overtly bloodied or broken. The S90 was lying on its side, the engine still running. There were a few marks, a mirror snapped off at the stalk, and the handlebars askew. We examined the triple-tree and forks, determined nothing important was bent, then straightened out the bars and continued on our way.

It was not until years later, after I'd heard the old biker adage, "You've never really ridden one until you've been down on it," that I realized the significance of this fairly unique achievement: my first bike, and I'd ridden and been down on it in the space of only three hours.

The S90 wasn't around very long. I rode it the rest of the summer, had another accident and nearly one more. I was pulling away from a stoplight, popped the clutch inadvertently, pulled a wheelie and almost brought it back on top of me. A nearby motorist yelled out his window. "You better learn how to ride that thing, bud!"

There were two basic flaws in the S90, or any other bike of its size. It was underpowered and under-braked, both of which would be immediately evident to anyone who would consider having one, except for somebody who knew practically nothing about motorcycles. Like me. At best, with nobody else on it, it might do 65 mph, and that would be downhill. With a passenger, it wouldn't do even that.

Whereas the advantages of a real motorcycle are speed, acceleration and maneuverability and in most normal circumstances being able to come to a controlled stop on your proverbial dime, with a scooter you can hardly do any of these. It's the main reason, along with not paying attention, why so many inexperienced and over-assuming riders get into jams on them.

One of the last times I rode the S90 was an unusually warm day in February of '66, the day we buried my father. He'd had a massive coronary, lingered on for a couple of days and then succumbed. "This is a rough one, Fritz," were the last words I remember him saying as I sat by his hospital bed.

At the wake, held at our home, I hung around for an hour or two, commiserated with friends and relatives over ham sandwiches, beans and salad, then without excusing myself went downstairs to the ground level and rolled out the Honda. The cemetery was but a block away, a little downside of our hill. I paused by his grave, dirt still fresh in the hole, and cried uncontrollably. I made a vow, I felt so bad, that I never again would allow myself to get so close to another human being, or they to me, that their passing would leave me so heartbroken. It was many years before I managed to move beyond that, and sometimes I still wonder if I really have. I hope so.

My father was a good man—honest, strong, a lieutenant in the Army artillery, world-class speed skater and coach, and extremely hard-working for the relatively little money he ever earned. Best part of all is the way I was raised—he let me grow to be me.

I wheeled the S90 away from the cemetery, and took a long, cool ride. Somehow, it made me feel better.

6

The White Madonna

By the time late spring of '66 rolled around, I traded in the 90 on Honda's next intermediate model—the CB Sport 160.

It was barely bigger than the 90, but the marginally larger engine, 161cc, delivered perceptibly more power. I owned it for less than a year, although long enough to come peeling out from a spot across the street from Jingles at bar time one night and up the hill past the old Randall School on Regent Street, hitting 85 mph. Traffic was all but nonexistent: No one but no one but me—and a cop in a cruiser, lurking on a side street, who clocked me. I forget the amount of the fine, but was worth six bad points of the 12 you got each year in Wisconsin before they pulled your license.

It was late the next winter when I wandered into a hole-in-the wall shop on Henry Street, pursuing a 305 Super Hawk, aka CB77, another Honda, which I was told by the owner—a beefy gearhead in a white T-shirt—had been "raced at Daytona." I had no reason to disbelieve him.

For all I knew, it had won a Grand Prix at Silverstone or on the moon, for that matter. I liked it—all white, a 305 cc engine with nearly twice the cubic centimeters of the 160, a 51-inch wheel base, and a decent road-holding weight of 350 pounds. It could cruise all day at 75 mph, reach out to 100 or a little better, and if you were to lie down over the tank to cut your wind resistance, crank it to full throttle and hang on tight for a mile, it could scare the bejeezus out of you.

The Super Hawk had a fairing, a solid testament, I was certain, that it must have been raced, although soon after purchase I removed it because in those days, except for true racers, they weren't all that cool. Most of us rode without windshields. I didn't know it at the time—in fact, I wouldn't read the book until later—that it was the same model Honda that Robert Pirsig rode on his fabled trip from Minnesota to California when he wrote *Zen and the Art of Motorcycle Maintenance* in 1974.

I assigned my own mythos by dubbing it *The Motorcycle White Madonna Two-Wheeled Gypsy Queen*, a take-off on a bike referred to by Bob Dylan in his 1965 recording, "Gates of Eden."

As a point of order, far as a fairing or windshield went, we weren't riding that far. Essentially, I rode as a "café racer," a British term from the '50's for fast and nimble but not all that large bikes, like the legendary Vincent Black Shadow, that were ridden hell-bent-for-leather from pub to club down shady country roads never designed for such foolishness. It was one of those, as I understand, a predecessor, on which T.E. Lawrence met his demise some years after sowing the seeds of his legend as Lawrence of Arabia.

Touring bikes were fairly rare. There were the huge Harley 74s, some of them formerly belonging to police highway patrols, the German-made 600- and 750cc BMWs, and Italian bikes, which were the class of the genre.

The Super Hawk, with barely half of the engine displacement of a Hog or its European betters, was no slouch, but definitely had to take a back seat in top speed to anything bigger. At speeds over 75-80, it wasn't very comfortable, but neither were any of the others. Until the late '90s, early 2000's, when Harley came up with its rubber-mounted Evolution engine, they vibrated and shook like used Maytags. "Washing Machine Charlies" we used to call them, paying backhanded homage to a certain model of Japanese bomber that in 1942 made nightly runs over Guadalcanal.

Those of us who rode Hondas or other Japanese bikes were in the minority. In American lore it was the Harleys, first produced in 1903, which were the unchallenged kings; the Indians, although no longer manufactured by then, were also of legend. They were not without challenge, however. In my neck of the woods, the Triumphs and BSAs, 500- and 650cc, outnumbered the Harleys and BMWs, and the Italian bikes were rarely seen. The Japanese bikes, or "rice burners" as they soon became known, sucked hind teat.

I've always been a Honda guy for the usual reasons. They were the first manufacturer to introduce bikes, or scooters, for inexperienced newbies, which were not so large to be intimidating. I felt reasonably assured on one. In fact, it was not until I bought the nearly 900-pound Valkyrie that I ever owned a bike so heavy that if I were to drop it, which everyone sooner or later will do, that I couldn't get it back up by myself.

A second reason is they were cheaper, and on what has turned into a life-long limited budget, something I could afford. The third reason, for which they are renowned, is their dependability. I can take care of bikes in the basics—changing oil, checking tire pressure and wear, monitoring fluid levels and making minor adjustments, but I've never been a "wrench" who can strip down a carburetor, replace a nicked gear or change a stator. For this, people like me, Hondas are nearly foolproof; folks like me as the fools.

Harleys are notoriously problematic, even the new ones, and parts replacements and labor are hellishly expensive. BMWs, for all their Teutonic engineering and refinements, cost just as much. In owning seven Hondas over 45 years (the fifth, an '86 700, I had only briefly, having bought it for Mar, my wife at the time, who decided she wasn't that nuts about riding it), the only part I've consistently had to replace is the stator, a combination of generator/alternator, which on most Hondas through the '80s habitually burned out. Otherwise, no major repairs. My '85 Shadow 1100 has 67,000 original miles on it, and it's never required any serious engine work, not even a valve job.

The times I spent on the Super Hawk were the highlight of my early riding. (The true halcyon days did not occur until more than 30 years later on the Shadow.) It was the late '60s and I was finishing college at UW, having skidded through over six years on what I referred to as the "12 Semester Plan." I never cared for it much, enrolled and persevered chiefly because I thought I'd better. You know—high school, military, college, job, marriage, baby, house, the path to stability in chasing the American Dream. I matriculated with a Gentleman's 2.4 GPA, majoring in Tomfoolery.

Toward the end of my college days, I lived in a rental house with my cousin, Augie, and our mutual friend, Larry. Augie had a Super Hawk like mine, only black, and Larry another Honda, huge for its time, a CB450 known in the industry as the "Black Bomber."

Larry had been riding longer than me or Augie. His previous bike was a Harley, which he was riding out west on University Avenue one afternoon when the motorist ahead of him stopped suddenly. Larry didn't, until the front of his bike collided with the rear of the car. Larry went over the top, literally, landing on his head and wearing no helmet. Fortunately, it happened in front of a dental office. The dentist came running out, coaxed him back to life, and Larry spent weeks in the hospital recovering. I doubt the fact that the accident had anything to do with the Harley, but the next time out, left largely in one piece and ready for another bike, he chose the Black Bomber.

The Bomber was bigger and heavier with a larger engine and more horsepower, but although its top speed was slightly better than ours, it was a little sluggish in acceleration. Since both Augie and I were lighter in weight, as were our bikes, we could run with Larry consistently without having him disappear into the sunsets. On occasion, Apple, who'd bought an S90 of her own, would join us.

Apple was my best friend. We were married five years.

For the most part, we'd ride the hills west of Madison, although usually not much farther than the Baraboo Range, adjacent to Lake Wisconsin and not far from the Dells. We rarely ventured farther than, say, a 60-mile radius. This is mostly what the geologists refer to as the "terminal moraine," which is country in which the glacier halted, then began to recede, leaving behind a landscape of low rolling hills and fertile valleys dotted with woodlands and perceptible clumps of large rocks and stones.

One of these, the Van Hise Rock, lies at the outskirts of a tiny burg called Rock Springs, just west of the Range on State 136. Discovered and chipped by the UW geologist Charles Van Hise in the first quarter of the 20th Century, it proved to scientifically demonstrate that the region once was a shallow sea, Pre-Cambrian as the geologists say, which eventually evolved into a mountain range. This was from 1.7 to 1.6 billion years ago. It was approximately 15,000 years ago that the glacier came along, leading in turn to what today is Devil's Lake and Lake Wisconsin, among the most scenic areas in southern Wisconsin. Or anywhere else, for that matter.

On our rides, though, we all took it for granted.

It was around this time for me, however, that my early riding days came to a self-imposed suspension, one which would prove to be protracted.

One reason was that the state passed a helmet law (or "hemmits" as my old pal Bugs used to call them), which put the kibosh to the timeless bikers' appeal of having the wind, rain and bugs in your hair (face and "teef"—another Bugsism) and required us by fiat to "protect ourselves" by covering up.

Nobody liked the law, save for the lawmakers.

The early helmet designs were relatively crude, wind-blown, noisy and confining; as mentioned, they cut off peripheral vision, and perhaps more importantly, restricted what you could hear. No doubt, especially today, helmets have a place and are designed much better, but when you were used to riding without them, what you could see or sense at the edges of your view, or what you could or couldn't hear–a car approaching on your left, preparing to pass, posed a dramatic change, even a challenge. I don't think it was more than a matter of months in having to wear one that a good part of the magic went out of my rides.

Ultimately, however, it was my recognition of mortality that got me out of the saddle.

I was coming into Madison from the west one afternoon, just outside of Middleton on State 14, and found myself entering a flat stretch with no traffic in sight. I cranked it. This is where a speedometer may lie, but as I leaned forward on the tank, eyes level with the handlebars, the speedo climbed to someplace close to 115. Likely, it wasn't that fast, given speedo error, maybe no more than 105, but it was fast enough. It was then, in a brief moment of enlightenment, when I thought about something, anything, that might perchance to pick that particular moment in its otherwise random existence to waddle out into my path.

A skunk, I recall, is what I pictured.

Damn, said I. Here I am, hurtling through time and space on two wheels and an engine: The Motorcycle White Madonna Two-Wheeled Gypsy Queen, and that at a time not long removed from Dylan's infamous crash at Woodstock, ostensibly caused by his "rear tire locking," which many of us later interpreted as the Bard of Hibbing jamming on his rear brake too hard.

Not long after, I sold the Hawk; don't even remember the circumstances or who bought it. Barely one year later, I was out of college, working a full-time job, and was married to Apple. A couple years after that came a baby.

There now were other considerations, important things, and riding a motorcycle 100 miles an hour, stimulating as it was, was not high on the list.

7

ME AND MY SHADOWS

The Driftless Area

1971-Present

The Shadow.

8

Back In the Saddle

For 25 years, not riding, I'd only dream of motorcycles.

It was a recurrent dream, though probably not as frequent as your average standards:

I'm back in the Navy, at sea, usually on the *Iwo Jima*, a helicopter carrier on which I served in the early '60s, we're in a storm, the ship is rolling and pitching, I'm trying to get from here to there and so forth; the standard, "I'm still in school, there's a test I didn't find out about until only now, I haven't studied and I'm going to be totally phuqued; and "I have a deadline," (ever popular among writers) "I'm rushing to meet it and there are obstacles."

In the motorcycle dream, usually brief but recurring all those years, I'd be at the top of a hill going down, but since I hadn't ridden for so long, I wasn't sure I remembered how. So I'd coast. I'd hang on to the bars, stick my legs out to the sides and roll down the hill. In its way, it was exhilarating.

I was a journalist most of those years—steady gigs at newspapers, articles for papers and magazines and forays into other areas, freelancing what I called "commercial work," that ran from public relations pap to "white papers" to children's books, radio, TV and paid consulting gigs. I was one of two guys who started a weekly newspaper, *Isthmus of Madison* as originally called, which is now approaching its 37th year of publication.

By '89, having frittered away so many words and the future in dubious undertakings that invariably left me wondering where the next month's rent was coming from, I finally took a job as a writer and editor for a nonprofit fundraising organization serving the University of Wisconsin.

We were living on Madison's near east side, three-and-a-half miles from the job, which in moderate weather I often would walk, taking a bus in the winter. We had only one car—a Ford Escort—and Mar often was using that. We talked about having an option.

"Why don't you buy a motorcycle?" asked Mar one day. "You used to ride."

Schwing!

I was on it like a fly, scarcely believing my ears. I mean, whose wife suggests that you buy a motorcycle?

I started looking around. Something used for sure, but something clean and spiffy. I'd lost track of all but everything, new designs, innovations and such, but recalled that back in '83 I'd seen a magazine ad showing Honda's latest, the Shadow 750. It was sleek-looking cruiser, a Harley clone, if you must, but with a shaft drive and liquid-cooled V-Twin contrasted to Harley's belt drive and air-cooled engine.

Investigating this bike nearly 10 years after it was produced, I found that other Japanese manufacturers had their versions, too—Yamaha, Kawasaki and Suzuki—and to my unpracticed eye, they all looked purty much the same. If there was one difference I knew, it was the Shadow was a Honda.

Some weeks later, I saw a newspaper ad. Somebody in Mount Horeb had one for sale. He'd just bought a boat and found he no longer had time for the bike. I went out there with a fella I'd met who knew more about bikes than I did, and we scouted it out: candy apple red, chrome front fender, low mileage, clean as a pussy cat's arse. A week later, I bought it.

It took a while, but before long I was starting to feel comfortable, at least as much as I'd been on the other bikes years before. I'd never really taken a lesson, short of the three hours in which Fiscus broke me in, so what I knew about riding was limited to my own proclivities and a few thousand miles of experience.

There still was a great deal to learn, and it wasn't until a few weeks later, when I took the Motorcycle Safety Foundation's basic rider safety course, that I really began to have a working idea of what I was doing. That is, there was plenty I'd been doing that wasn't right, and lots more I'd never been shown or just happened to stumble upon those few years I'd been riding in the '60s.

A lot of it is little stuff, much of it rather natural if you once get a clue, but things you really should know very well, the kind that are important to file away in your brain, and which eventually become embedded into your consciousness, nerves and muscles.

When you're turning, turn your head exaggeratedly in the direction you want to go. Miraculously, the bike will follow your lead. When coming to a stop or taking off, keep your head up, eyes ahead. This will overcome the tendency, which I still see among neophytes, to swerve a bit and wobble, looking down or aside, not really taking time to point your face in the direction you'd like the bike to be going. Reduce speed going into a curve, set your "line" like race drivers do, entering high, slicing low at the midpoint, then going high again, accelerating as you exit.

Simple stuff, some of the basics, but invaluable to know. The more you ride, the more you learn, goes a saying, and this true. But if you're smart enough to get in on the groundwork, learning the basics, chances are better you'll ride safer and longer with a clear-cut margin of greater success.

'Course, this doesn't make you foolproof. Not by far. Shit still happens, sometimes having nothing to do whatsoever with either your mistakes, lack of attention or even well-intended volition.

The only accident I had on the 750 was one afternoon at rush hour, riding home from work on a three-lane, one-way street, farthest lane to the right, when this woman in the lane to my left decides she wants to turn. I'd been watching her closely, even checking her eyes in her rearview mirror, but damn, she nailed me anyway.

She turned right in front of me across two lanes, no signal; I tried to lean the bike along with her, edging along a few feet from her front fender until finally she closed and gave me a nudge at her door; we went bump and she knocked me over. There was damage, not irreparable but costly, and I had another bruised knee and a big slice cut out of my best set of dress pants.

The 750 was a run-up for me. In the 25 years I hadn't ridden, a lot of changes had been made. And the 750 when I bought it already was almost 10 years old. Mostly, it had to do with handling and power.

The handling on the 750 was decent, better than the Super Hawk, which handled well enough for its time, but by comparison had a way of plowing its way through corners. The Shadow was sleek, fast and nimble—not terribly fast, but with six gears, the last essentially an overdrive, it could cruise a highway briskly, if not always in comfort, for about as long as you had gas.

Mostly, it was on an interstate that it really showed its limits. The sixth gear could carry you along all day at 3,500 rpm and 75 mph, but if you wanted to goose it from there, say, a passing situation, there wasn't all that much gander in the goose. This was especially true if I was riding two-up, Mar on the back. Toss in a little luggage, weighing the ass end of it down, and we were talking about the low side of power.

Not long after I bought it, I started hunting around on the Internet for more information, other folks who rode them. This led me to a Shadowriders website, which was run out of Plano, Texas. In time, not all that long, the folks who were running it passed on server responsibilities to a woman in Indiana. Not long after that, it became the project of Marc Mauss, a New Yorker, biker, and MSF safety instructor whose day job is in the electronics biz. He had a Shadow

1100, two or three over time, counting spare parts as many as four or five, and a feel and a knack for the growing potential of social interaction online.

A list member named Dawg in Chicago suggested he'd like to see a site in which folks could wander in at their leisure, order up a cyberdrink, lean back on the bar and share with everybody else the experiences of the day, the week, the trip they took over the weekend. In effect, with the support and enthusiasm of a growing group of participants, the site became the "Roadhouse," a virtual bar, predominantly for Shadow riders but all bikers welcome, who clicked in from all over the country, some from other parts of the world.

That's a story in itself. The cast of characters was colorful, diverse and classic, some like you'd find nowhere else. Everybody had a handle, and as time progressed, personalities evolved in and around it, so that we developed a fairly broad yet personal picture, a movie, of who we were and what each of us brought to the table.

There was Merlin—Marc Mauss—who I somehow couldn't keep (and still can't) from calling Maussie; Bugs, who was so much more but who got his name for a biochemical application he had spent a good deal of time seeking to nurse to fruition—synthetic microbes that he would cultivate and introduce commercially into landfills so they would eat all the garbage and trash; and the Shaggy Wierdo (sic), a thinker, diarist and man of salty letters, often descriptive of bodily fluids and expulsions, who might best be described in one's cyber image as coming off something like The Thing from that '50s horror movie starring James Arness.

There was Dawg, Torque, Slick, the Deer Slayer, Sulli, Barkeep, Fre, Old Fogey, Foxee, wiLld BiLL, the Rev. Roadkill, Hogkiller, Sarge, Pops and Hollyshockz and a dozen more who me poor ol' addled brain can't now begin to remember. It was our own private/public clubhouse, and at the height of our party, we had a daily/nightly crowd of a good 15-20 regulars and several score others lurking or hanging around. The high membership, as I recall, was over 100.

I was "Unca Freddie." Times that I drop in, still am.

It went on for several years, starting in the early '90s, and is still in operation today at *shadowriders.org*. But for some of us, mostly old-timers, it eventually started to play itself out. Bugs died, for one, and he was a catalyst. He could turn almost any subject into a philosophical, political, historical or theological discussion, and he was funny to boot. Part Turk, part Cherokee, mostly Scotch, a North Carolinian by birth and living in Alabama, a Marine vet of the 'Nam, a college grad with time in law school, a former cop, town alderman and an executive officer of the Sons of Confederate Veterans motorcycle club, Bugs was a pistol. In those days at the House, with people like this, anything went.

There were almost no taboos, and amidst all the b.s. and laughs, invaluable information was passed back and forth about the bikes we rode, how to best ride and fix them. Intellectually, humorously, often emotionally, even spiritually, we all prospered for it.

Rest his soul, Bugs got out first, taking gravely ill and dying soon after, in fact, before membership broadened and with it, the inexorable rise of PC, oozing its way in, undermining with misplaced earnestness and only the narrowest sense of what's funny or not, what's "appropriate," the very foundation, ruining the whole goddamn concept of what we wanted and loved about the House. I mean, imagine a biker hangout that is politically correct. Sensing it coming, I bugged out, too.

Before I left, however, I found my next bike: a 1985 Shadow 1100, nearly cherry when I bought it, and along with the Valk, still sitting proud and perky in my garage today.

9

Donner und Blitzen

One of the first things I learned in the Roadhouse is that for Shadow riders the bike to have was the 1100C, '85-86 models. When I'd toot about my 750, someone would invariably say, "Wait until you get on the big one. You'll never go smaller again."

That was intriguing.

In the early '80s (whilst I slept) Honda had launched, in what inappropriately might be called a surprise attack, a new marketing strategy to revolutionize the American market. Within the space of three years, they introduced not one, not two, but three landmark motorcycles: the Shadow, Magna and Sabre.

The Shadow, an affordable, state-of-the market V-Twin cruiser with a none-too-original but acceptable style (see Harley) cloaking a deceptively mean set of cojones, was perhaps the most modest of the three. The Magna had a larger frame, still in the cruiser category but in support of its more powerful V4 engines (750cc and 1100cc) presenting the look of a taller, husky, broad-shouldered beast, which it soon proved to be on the road.

For a time, it was a run-off between the Magna and challengers put forth by Yamaha and Suzuki to see who could build an ostensible cruiser that could go fastest in a quarter mile (and reliably in a straight line, because cornering was never their strong suit). The Sabre, with essentially the same V4 engines but markedly different in overall style, was what we might classify today as a mid-sized "sport bike" or "rocket," streamlined with a small fairing, and at the far edge of that, a seminal forerunner to today's sport tourers.

The Sabres came and went; there are still original Magnas today, beloved by their owners, but nowhere near so many as might have been, because they were just so damn fast they scared the shit out of people.

By the early '90s, Honda had gone through several years of refinements on their Shadow line, but not all of them an improvement. The second 750 Shadow, sub-named the ACE, remains a great bike today, whereas the ACE 1100s, although attractive for the purpose of longer-range cruising, were not built for exceptional speed, and gas mileage was poor. By the late '80s, the Shadows had been reduced to only four gears, a poor modification that Honda chose to continue, and worst of all, they eventually dumbed down the horsepower.

This was either to appease the emissions Nazis or a misbegotten effort to gear them back to what they considered a safer riding level for the fast-rising middle-aged American cruiser market, mostly middle-aged men. Eventually, they all but emasculated them, the bikes, that is, turning out a whole and continuing line with but 47 woebegone horses in the innards.

The '85-86's were designed and produced with 78 horse—no performance kits necessary, no tinkering—right out of the box. For a 585-pound bike and 1099cc, only a couple hundred cubic centimeters short of Harley's Big Twin, it was the first Japanese bike to produce that large of an engine displacement. This was a bike made to run with the big boys.

By the time I caught on to them, they already were rare. Not nearly so rare as they are today, wherein you can hardly find one, even parts, but by the mid-'90s purty well snapped up and kept primo by connoisseurs. And whereas your average Harley in those days still cost a half arm and leg, the 1100C Shadows originally retailed for around $4,000. Ten years later, when I got mine, I paid $3,200.

I found it through the Roadhouse. A fella in Florida, Vince Santamaria, was a House member and a guy we knew who kept his bikes well, took great care of them, and often had three or four in his stable. He'd come upon this one down there, it had been stored most of its life and had only 7,500 original miles on it, about half of which Vince had put on since he bought it.

We chatted back and forth. I trusted his honesty and with that his judgment and wound up buying it sight unseen, shipped to Wisconsin for around 200 bucks. It came in original colors—black with gray fenders—and the only mod being a crossover exhaust system he had installed, straight shorty pipes with no baffles, to replace the side-by-side stocks.

I picked it up at Madison Motorsports, the shop I'd been favoring for work on the 750. Within short order, I had it repainted all black and dubbed it *Donner und Blitzen*, "Thunder and Flash" (or "lightning," if you will).

There was a good deal about it, innovations that Honda created, that I didn't understand very well then and still don't. But essentially, it featured refinements to the fork and suspension that reduced vibration, and with it customer savings by not having to rubberize the engine mounting. Honda also put in a hydraulic clutch assisted by a three-way operational system combining the spring, oil from the engine and centrifugal force to create greater pressure on the plate yet at the same time spreading the load. They also tweaked both the spark and ignition systems.

I learned all this later. Don't give me a test.

What I did know, however, is that I liked it. A lot. For the first time, I had a powerful highway cruiser, easy to handle, still not too heavy but enough to battle crosswinds, and extremely dependable. Did I say dependable? In 17 years, about all the work it's ever needed was a new carb and a stator, which finally burned out only two years ago. I replaced it with a heavy-duty model, which I'm quite sure will outlast me.

The only other thing that went wrong was the choke cable broke early on, and that happened to be on a day when my mechanic was riding it. Other than tires and two or three windshields before I finally found one I liked, that and a battery I once burned out through neglect, it has never needed repair.

Oh, wait. There was one other time.

Mar and I were on a weekend ride to the Mississippi and the inland bluffs and hill country running north and south between La Crosse and Eau Claire. We'd rented a motel room in Arcadia, and for the next couple days we rode the winding roads through hills and valleys, woodlands, farm land and ridges. We stopped off in Trempealeau, the old hotel and its veranda at riverside overlooking the Minnesota bluffs, and then for an early evening nightcap, we rode to Bluff Siding for a quick stopover at a gin mill and strip club I'd happened upon sometime before. To get there, we followed a narrow winding trail called Chicken Ranch Road. It was owned by a bike club out of Eau Claire, and for some curious zoning reason their clubhouse was right next to the bar.

It was around 6 p.m., and as I motored confidently into the parking lot, the Shadow started spewing oil. It was coming out of the left side, stopped when I turned off the switch, but continued to drip. I didn't know what it was, but I knew we were temporarily phuqued. It was a Saturday night, no one within 1,000 miles was going to help us until Monday, and there we were.

I approached the managers humbly, asking if I might lean the bike against the side of their clubhouse until arranging a tow on Monday morning. They were magnanimous, for which I was grateful, if somewhat apprehensive nevertheless, for the last time I'd been there—a big party for Vietnam Vets—they'd filled a Kawasaki with gas (representative Japanese rice burner), stacked it on top of a tall wooden pyre, then set fire to the wood. At the point the flame reached the gas tank, the bastid exploded and the crowd, which was considerable, cheered mightily.

Through the friendship of Foxee, an old Roadhouse pal who drove 120 miles round-trip to retrieve us, we were schlepped back to our motel where for the next three days we waited for a parts truck from the Quad Cities to motor up the Mississippi to Whitehall, a regional Honda shop where the bike had been hauled. Turned out to be a small part in the slave cylinder, a $2.70 rubber gasket.

I wrote a song about the three days in Arcadia, a bluesy biker's lament with a chorus about watching other bikers cruise up and over the hill on nearby State 93 all day and night, but I can't find the lyrics any more. I did sent a note to the bike club, thanking them profusely for their consideration, not in the least in not burning my bike, and added sincerely that if I ever got by that way again, I'd polish their boots.

When healthy, which has been most of the time, the Shadow is very fast. Except for a year or two when in my density I went around with half a bum carb, it runs as well today as the day it was made. I'm not into racing, and the older I get the easier, more relaxing it is to loaf along just above the speed limit, but there was a time early on when I pushed it. How fast would it go?

The speedo reads 130, and in chatting with the Roadies at the House, a couple of them said they had coaxed theirs close to that number. I wanted to find out. So one day, can't remember where or when, I found a long, clear stretch of road with no one around, flattened down over the tank and gave her full crank. I took it to 100 in fourth gear, shifted up to fifth, and at about 115 mph felt a shudder, sort of like I was going through a sound barrier. It came out of the shudder at 118 and I stuck with it all the way to 123. That's what the speedo said, anyway.

Plenty fast enough.

These days, in my dotage, I rarely get up over 80–85. If I do, and Barbi, m'lady, is in back, I get elbows to the ribs.

10

Mortality

A lot of folks think riding a bike is dangerous. Most motorcyclists understand there's a risk. Accidents and injuries are commonplace. There's no thin veneer of metal or plastic between you and the road, a rock, stone fence, tree or a ditch. Even under the best of conditions, glimpses of mortality flee by often and quickly.

I have always been aware of this, and it played a huge role in my extended absence from riding. Eventually, driven by whatever ails me, I got to the point where I felt I'd grown old enough, pushing 60, to where I didn't give so much of a damn anymore.

My pal Moonie and I have a greeting, hello and goodbye, something I copped from the Sioux, their war cry as they rode into battle: *Hoka hei!* —"It's a *good* day to die!"

I was living in New Glarus, a village of 2,000 in the heart of Wisconsin's cheese and dairy tradition, 30 miles south of Madison. On a Memorial Day weekend, I invited seven friends for a little rally, a ride through the lower leg of the Driftless Area and the hills flanking the valleys of the Wisconsin River and plain.

We were on our way back after a trip that had taken us through the Baraboo Range and a cut-back down past Taliesin, the Frank Lloyd Wright estate near Spring Green. We had just come off the river and were climbing a steep curvy hill on State 130 north of Dodgeville. Riding staggered, one-by-one so there was room to spare should any of us have to maneuver, we approached a tight left-hander, just moseying along, when around the curve with the sun at its back comes a motor home.

It's lumbering, swaying, arse-end hanging over the yellow line, and had we not corrected, it would have been a mess. Best we might have got out of it was to take to the bush and the trees, tumbling down hill. Instead, instinctively, we all swung oblique to the right, then came back out of it same as we were going in. At the next stop, however, you may be sure it was the leading topic of conversation.

Another time, my pal Moonie and I were chasing each other around Green County, heading home on State 69, and on a flat stretch leading up the hill to the New Glarus Woods. We looked around to see who was watching, nobody was, so we jacked it. Moonie was riding his Excelsior-Henderson, a big and powerful bike, nearly 1800cc after some tweaking, and I was on *Donner und Blitzen.*

I trailed him closely until three-quarters of the way up the rise and then I shifted to fifth, 100 mph, and the Shadow surged, pulling alongside. We had just crested the hill when—ping!—something caromed of my windshield and flew past my ear.

I thought it was a stone, something lying in the road, but at the same time I detected a metallic ring. In an instant *D&B* started to shimmy, then wobble, and I quickly floundered, losing speed, as Moonie disappeared around the next curve and down into the valley.

I was fast losing front tire pressure—in essence a flat, if not yer dreaded blowout. I hobbled along for the next mile, caught up to Moonie at the main intersection in town, and by this time was riding on the rim. We inspected. That ping I'd heard was a valve stem cap that had flown off the tire. It had sheared off clean at the base and turned into a missile.

Reason was, the caps I had on there were not stock; that is, not long before, I had purchased an after-market set done up to look like the empty cartridges of a .357. You've seen other ones—dice, skulls, that sort of thing—but the mitigating factor here is that their excess length and weight had caused the rubber valve stem at even normal speeds to spin with the tire and bend violently, doubled-back I suppose, until at this particular juncture, it had flat broken off.

The good news was that by breaking off even with the rim, the pressure in the tire escaped gradually. Had it all gone at once, blown at the crest of that hill and all else being equal, I would have lost control of the bike and been launched over the handlebars, something like a monkey in a rocket, high enough over the Little Sugar River Valley that I'd have a birds-eye view of the State Capitol in downtown Madison, 35 miles away.

And no, I wasn't wearing a hemmit.

There's one line of thought, heard from time to time among trail-savvy bikers, and that is there are some days you wake up feeling frisky, planning for a ride, start getting your gear together, but from somewhere down deep, uninvited, there comes a lurking, nagging feeling, usually vague, that for some reason something doesn't feel quite right, that maybe you shouldn't be riding that day.

I've rarely had those, but on occasion I have. It's hard to pinpoint. Physically, on the whole mentally, I may be feeling okay, but something troubling, though undefined, is ragging me. Sometimes it might even be something you read, a story you hear, a harrowing incident that strikes a note and sticks in your head.

While edging into the fall of one otherwise fine riding season, I touched base one night with someone I hadn't seen for months, a close old buddy I'd known for 20 years. He'd been lying low, nary to be seen for several months, so it was not until over a couple of beers and a bitters and lime at a Willy Street bistro that learned that several months before he'd been in a serious accident, nearly buying the farm. It was in a car, driving back from his hometown in western Wisconsin where he'd visited family and partied with friends.

The country between there and Madison is characterized by long straight stretches traversing high ridges, then curving tightly, intermittently dipping down into narrow valleys and hollows cut through thick woods. In high spirits, 4 a.m., my buddy was traveling fast. Too fast. He overshot a curve and lost control. The car left the road, rolled down an embankment, flipped over and landed topside first on a line of fencing, my bud hanging upside down by the seatbelts. Then it flipped again, finally coming to rest on all four wheels.

He sat stunned for a few moments, then began to clear his senses. He looked around. There was a jagged metal hole in the roof, the mark of an iron post that had punctured and penetrated during the initial landing. It was a foot from his head.

Badly shaken but ambulatory, bleeding from a gash to his forehead, he crawled up the hill and hitchhiked for help.

I didn't dwell on it—thought hearing it once was plenty enough—but it certainly left an impression. I consigned it to the keep locker—something I shouldn't forget.

11

Down to the Crossroads

It was one of those days when everything else felt right except for a hint of that deep nagging discomfort.

On the cool side but clear and sunny, *Donner und Blitzen* was ready to roll. I took off from Madison around noon, an area I usually didn't ride, taking me away from the Driftless Area and north into Columbia County. It's mostly broad valleys, rich farmland flanked in the distance by low rolling hills, not so high as country to the west, generally flat by comparison and speckled with small patches of woodlands.

The bike was running very well, temp in the low '60s, which opposed to having the carbs labor to suck hot, humid air, tends to make all things run better, the engine sing and the bikes go faster. You can get on top of your rpm in whatever gear you happen to be in and you can ride it right there, holding it steady with a slight jig of the throttle, and you can feel and hear the engine running at maximum efficiency. It's like you're sitting on top of the revs. You give it a crank and the bike leaps forward with a deep throated snarl, the sound of the engine and mufflers, the harmonics, come close to achieving the divine.

So here I was on County C, cruising along in the sunshine, and the further I got, the less I was troubled, whatever had ailed me fading into the recesses and now approaching a stage of mild bliss. I became much more relaxed, tuned in to the road and surrounding environment, leaning back into the pocket of the seat, feet up on the highway pegs, sucking in big breaths of fresh air and enjoying the view. But I still kept my focus, intrinsically aware. Bliss be damned, you never know when some dumb shit will come along to do something stupid.

The road I was riding was new to me, miles north of where I'd ridden it before, and one of its unexpected delights was a series of tight little curves snaking along for a couple of miles through the flatness. Had I been familiar with them, known the angles, I might have gone into them harder. But these were uncharted and angled tight, cast here and there with patches of washed-out gravel and dirt.

Best instead to ease off, take 'em cautious, circumnavigate. The last was a 45-degree right-hander, banked down toward the inside, with a line of this loose wash running down the center through the midpoint of the turn. Easing back, I skittered on through without a twitch or a twiddle. The road straightened out and again I settled back.

I'd hardly encountered any other cars. Only twice in several miles did I see so much as one, each time crossing other county roads, and I stopped at the signs as it might occur, letting them pass. The next intersection, County CF running east and west, was a quarter-mile ahead. A fair piece out on my left, perpendicular, there was a van heading east. He wasn't going fast; seemed in fact to be slowing down as he approached the only sign, which was his.

I don't have one, a stop sign, that is. But since it's a four-way intersection and I'm lugging along in fourth gear at 50 mph and about to cross a railroad track, I drop it into third, then second and roll it back to 25. The van is almost to the intersection, I can see now that it's green, and he's doing, what, 10 to 15?

Well, the next thing I know, I am entering the intersection and much to my deep consternation, very sudden-like, so is he. He hasn't stopped. He's right phuquing there. He's a few yards away, coming at me, broadside from the port quarter.

There was no time to brake, not even to contemplate. A skid and a slide, brakes locked up, would have been likely and we still would have collided. I had one choice, and that was to give it all we got.

Now, at this point I 'd like to personally thank the engineers at Honda, some of them likely dead, who put this little bike together on the drawing board, and the guys in the factory when they cast the molds of that snappy V-Twin engine, and whoever else came along and dialed in so much torque that in damn near any gear you can give her a good old twist and she'll lift the front wheel when she takes off.

That's certainly true in first and second, anyway, and in the other three gears she ain't no slouch. A "torque monster" is the way it was described to me by a fella on a Ducati that spring, a guy familiar with the breed.

When Honda first built them, they weren't sure of what they had to do with this sort of bike to sell it in America, so I've been told, but what they finally came up with is something that looks like a cruiser but underneath it has the soul of a sport bike.

Fact is, it was the torque that saved me arse. I was going through the crossroad, right of way, and the next thing I knew he was there, too, damn near right in the side of my face. I goosed it and she responded—*D&B* springing forth like some mystical mount, sweeping me on through the intersection and on up the road at a very brisk clip. Explosive, you might say. Only a split second before, I was fixin' to become a big bloody spot on this guy's grill. I had just enough time to holler out one good "god-damn!" and I was past.

I went on down the road a hundred yards or so with my eyes as big as wheel rims, and I shook my head like a dumb old dog right after you might bat him alongside of the head with a board, just to get his attention, and I then said aloud, "Damn! Did that really just happen?"

I sat at the side of the road for a moment, breathing hard, collecting myself. Next instant, I turned around and backtracked, hung a left at the intersection, glanced at a sign, and I was hauling hard up a hill called Messerschmidt Hollow, a road to the hills, blood pumping fast and giving hot chase. It took a few minutes because of the crossing roadways and winding terrain, but I caught him a couple miles later as he was pulling up to a stop sign. I backed it down into third, then second, rolled up behind him and laid on the horn.

He heard it, finished his turn and pulled over. I slid in next to him.

It was a little old man, wire-rimmed glasses, hearing aid in the left ear. He was wearing a brown suit, red bow tie, and from the looks I judged him to be 80, mebbe 85 years old. Sitting next to him, makin' not a peep, was the little woman. She was wearing a white flowered dress, Sunday-go-to-meetin' type.

I took in the picture pretty quick, and as the gods would have it, by the time I opened my mouth, I was completely rational. It was as though in a burst of latent understanding and compassion, all the bile burned right out of my gut.

I asked him if he knew what just happened back there. He allowed that he did. I asked if he knew he ran the stop sign, and he said no—he'd stopped, looked both ways, didn't see me, then started up again. And all of a sudden, he said, there I was, shooting across the road only a few feet in front of him. He said it shook him up, and that he still had the shakes.

They were on their way to a wedding in Columbus, and he was terribly sorry, there's no way he could apologize enough.

Wahl, that may all be well and good, I thought to myself, but if you'd care to get out and take a look at yer left front headlight, yer gonna find about an inch of me leathers and arse spread all over it, imprinted on the lens.

But I didn't say that. I didn't argue or yell. I just told him that was as close as I've ever come to checkin' out real quick on a bike, and maybe, just maybe, for the rest of the day, we could both go on about our business and try to be a little more aware of what we're doing out here. He nodded, that would be the prudent thing to do, and I reached through the window and shook his hand.

I rode on east to Columbus because that's where the road led me, and stopped at the first bar I could find with motorcycles parked out front—two Harleys and an old Triumph—and I pulled over and parked next to a green Electra Glide. The bar was called the Cardinal's Cage. I shut down the bike, got off and walked in. I ordered a double shot of Jack and a tap chaser, lit a cigarette and asked to borrow the phone. I dialed up my old buddy, the one who'd flipped his car and nearly bought the farm.

"You're not going to believe what just happened," I said.

He did, he does, and so do I.

12

Freddie Get Yer Gun

My early history with guns, I believe, is not appreciably different from most young American boys who grew up in the '50s.

I worshiped John Wayne, especially after seeing him in John Ford's epic Cavalry Trilogy, circa 1948–50. So distressed was I at *Rio Grande* when as Col. Kirby Yorke he catches an Apache arrow in the chest, that I had to be assured by my father in the seat next to me that the Duke would come out of it just fine.

I was a creature of the movies. My mother took me to comedies and musicals and my father to Westerns and adventure films. Often, the guys in the movies had guns.

But it wasn't just movies and Westerns. As a kid, I also read books: *King Arthur and the Knights of the Round Table, Ivanhoe, The Three Musketeers, Robin Hood, The Last of the Mohicans.* In all these dramatic portrayals of history, there were good guys and bad guys, and invariably when it came down to settling matters, great or small, they'd eventually turn to swords, knives, lances, spears, battle axes, tomahawks, bows and arrows and eventually guns to reach their denouement.

I found a thread here.

The late Col. Jeff Cooper, a retired Marine, made an astute observation.

Having come to renown as a combat veteran, gun expert and designer, instructor nonpareil, author of books and many articles about guns and their relative place and importance in society, he wrote, and I paraphrase:

If you don't understand weapons, you don't understand war. If you don't understand war, you don't understand history. If you don't understand history, you don't understand Man.

And if you don't understand Man, you might as well live with your head in a sack.

My father had guns, though not many. There was the .22 revolver he used as a starter's pistol, firing blanks in the air as the signal for his skaters to get their arses quick off the line, a 12-gauge Browning semi-automatic shotgun, and an 8mm German Mauser, *Karibiner 98k*, that a buddy had brought back from the war.

The shotgun he used for pheasant and rabbit, the Mauser for hunting deer. Whereas I found them intriguing, without his permission I wouldn't begin to think of taking them out and playing with them any more than I would to spit in his face. The pistol he kept in a dresser drawer, but the long guns were kept not in his closet, which he shared with my mother and had no space, but in mine, cased and unloaded in a corner beneath the rack of my dress shirts and pants.

Hunting, I never got into. There were times I'd go along with my father, stalking pheasant usually, but never showed that much of an interest and the old man didn't push it in turn. He did, however, teach me to shoot.

A crack shot despite his poor eyesight, he started me with a BB gun, a Daisy Red Ryder lever-action, and a Crossman pellet pistol. His instructions were simple: front sight on the target, stock tucked in tight to the shoulder, breath control, squeeze the trigger don't pull, and follow through on the shot by holding your line of sight steady down the barrel of the gun. It's only marginally different from a long gun to a pistol.

And, yes—always be sure if it's loaded or empty, and never point it at anybody unless you want to put out their eye.

As close as we ever got to slaughtering anything as a team was the odd starling or grackle squawking in our oak tree, or the gophers that dug up our lawn.

Pains to admit it, but we didn't kill none o' the critters jes' for the meat.

For a long while after that, guns had no great place in my life. I had two or three I'd casually acquired and been keeping around, but nothing of value except a single-shot Savage, over-and-under rifle and shotgun combo, .22 Mag over .20 gauge.

In '69, not long out of college, I bought it for squirrel hunting with some old high-school buddies. They hunted regularly, often on a farm west of Madison owned by one of the gang. Afterward, they'd gather at the house to skin and boil the spoils to remove what was left of the hair (most of it, anyway) and then piece them up for roast on the grill. They'd been pestering me to join them, it sounded like fun, so I went along on a hunt.

It was a bright fall morning. We paired off into twos, a dozen of us, and set off through the hills and the woods. I shot three or four squirrels with the .22. Then at one point I found myself at the top of a draw and down below was my partner working his way up. He rousted a squirrel.

Here it comes on the ground, darting and dodging, scurrying behind a tree. I look for my partner and he's off to the left, well out of my sweep. The squirrel gives me a head fake, peering out from his left, and then he breaks the other way and cuts out.

In a primordial instant I knew I'd never have a chance with the .22, so I switched the barrel-control lever to the .20 gauge and fired from the hip.

When we gathered our harvest, counted up and prepared them, this was the only one that was so mangled that it wasn't worth dropping into the pot.

Two weeks later, sitting under a tree in Vilas Park, a couple of blocks from where I was living in Madison, a very strange thing happened. I was leaning back, reading a book. It was peaceful and still, no one nearby. I hear this scratching sound, glance up the trunk to my left, and here's this squirrel, looking at me from about three feet away.

We looked at each other for a long time, holding our gaze with a silent but studied exchange of mutual accord, one living thing and another, and we came to terms. I return to my reading and he crawls back up the tree.

Wahl, I tell ya. After that, how could I even think about killing these things? Or most anything else, far as that goes. I took it seriously. I got to where I wouldn't even kill a spider. It wasn't long after that I sold all the guns.

This was in the mid-'70s, you see, and I'd come to a place, was seeking a place, in which I might live my life in some semblance of harmony and largely without hassle. I was seeking to become centered, and if I began to achieve that, if I even came close, I might possibly come into tune—with my family, loved ones and friends, people in general, the environment and the whole goddamn world, the universe, should it not first cave in on my head in sharp rejection of this remarkable metaphysical transformation.

As the elder comes to know, times change.

Instead of coming closer together, you name the inspirational source, we began to move further apart—speaking here of "we" in the universal sense. I hung in there for a while, believing in the ideal, but by the time I'd left Madison for life in Los Angeles and New York, mostly to see how the other halves lived, I came back with the hard-earned conviction that indeed it is a jungle out there.

And I'm not blaming L.A. or New York. They're only microcosms of the macrocosm.

Too many people began disregarding the most basic tenets of a civilized society, how to treat each other commonly with so much as the smallest nod of respect. At worst, we became ever more conscious of violence and fear, suspicion and distrust, and even at our best and most optimistic could not escape the creeping anxiety of knowing that none of us are immune.

Wahl, it changed for me, anyway—an incident in a 'burb, south side of Madison in the mid-'80s, that struck closely.

A woman is alone in the apartment. The husband's at work. She's reading, lying on the couch in the living room.

Somebody at the window, stalking through the shrubs, is peering in.

He enters the building, hall empty, and stops at her door. He turns the handle. It's unlocked, so he enters. He's standing in the kitchen, rummaging through a drawer, when she walks around the corner.

He grabs a knife and attacks.

In the struggle that ensues, he drags her into the bathroom, slashing her with the knife. He hits her, knocking her down, then shoves his hand in her mouth, his nails gouging her throat. He grabs her around the neck and strangles her into unconsciousness, then fearful of something—maybe she's dead—decides to get up and run for it. If not, say the cops later, he would have raped and probably killed her.

At work, the husband is called to the phone. He hurries home. There's blood on the walls of the kitchen, blood on the walls of the john. The wife is trembling, still in shock. The police and paramedics have been there and gone. Their advice is to be careful, more cautious, make sure the door is locked. You should take precautions, he may come again.

But for the wife and husband, however, their shock and pain, the consequences may never end.

For the next three nights, the hubby is outside the apartment, a wooded area next to the complex. He's dressed in dark clothing, a watch cap, and he's carrying a hunting knife and a three-quarter inch wrench. He's standing quietly in the shadow of a tree, praying that the guy will return.

Wahl, that got me to thinking.

I bought an old 16-gauge pump, a Mossberg clone sold by Monkey Ward in the '50s. I had the barrel sawed down, a legal 18.5 inches.

"Why do that?" asked a friend.

"So I don't knock over a lamp while I'm sweeping the room."

I tend to be glib, but this is serious stuff. I wish it were otherwise.

The shotgun, always a fave for home defense, led to a pistol, something I can carry outside the house. I don't always carry, but if heading downtown, traveling, and especially on the bike with m'lady, you betcha.

It is not always a pretty world. Shit does happen, and regardless of one's good faith and intentions, the random factor is ever in play.

Don't tread on me.

13

Wild Bill Fred

If there ever was a time on the bike when I really thought I might need a gun, it was a day when Barbi and I were out on the Shadow on a high ridge in western Wisconsin overlooking a series of lesser hills rolling away to the south. We'd stopped, parked the bike on the shoulder and got off to admire the view.

We were on State 33, not an untraveled road but a good piece from the New York Thruway. On this stretch, there was no other traffic, no other people, no houses or barns except those dotting the valleys below.

Around the curve comes a pick-up truck, slowing as it moves into sight. It stops next to us, not on the shoulder but the middle of the road. There's two young guys inside.

Seldom one to make snap judgments, give or take now and then, I make one here.

These guys are crackers.

The one wearing the ball cap leans out his window.

"Pretty nice bike."

"Thanks."

"That a Harley?"

"No, it's an old Shadow."

You'd think that ought to be enough, right? I mean, I wasn't up there to win a trophy. C'mon, it's a 15-year-old Honda. Ain't worth stealing.

But I'll be damned, the driver opens his door, hangs a leg over the side of the seat, and the guy riding gunner gets out. He walks around the front and stands next to the hood. Barbi can see into the cab, she tells me later, and there's trash and empties on the floor. They're giving us the twice-over, sort of casing the scene. Barbi gets a third look. They measure the odds.

Apparently, they weigh in our favor.

Why?

Whatever they had on their minds, someone had to be thinking, what if Gramps over there is carrying a gun? He looks as though he could be the type.

The air is still. I turn slightly to my left so they can see I have in my right hand a Smith & Wesson Model 686, .357 Magnum, the eight-inch barrel hanging long down my leg.

In the distance, a raven croaks. Turkey buzzards circle overhead.

"You folks have a nice day," says one of the crackers. Gunner hops back in the truck and they drive off.

Ha, ha. That's a joke. No raven, no buzzards, and I had no Six-Eighty-Six.

But here's an even better one.

I did have a gun but it was locked in my saddlebag.

At the time this took place, Wisconsin did not have a concealed carry law. It passed one in fall of 2011, leaving Illinois as the only state in the union to not have some sort of CC provision. If I wanted to carry a gun to stay within the law, I was subject to the same conditions as other motorists. I could carry a gun, although not on my person, and it had to be cased and unloaded, inaccessible to my reach, and that included the glove compartment, by the way.

The one exception, oddly enough, is that there is an open-carry law—you can carry one open—a law that's been on the books damn near since Wisconsin was part of the Northwest Territory. Trouble is, you can't carry it openly in a vehicle (figure that) and should you be carrying on the street, the right hip for instance, and somebody finds this alarming, they'll call a cop. The cop will take your gun and cite you for disturbing the peace. You'll lose the case, pay a fine and the police will give back your gun whenever they're good and ready.

To comply, good citizen that I yam, I carried the gun in a saddlebag. It was a Ruger SP-101, and not only was it unloaded and locked in a case (a couple of speed loaders tucked in the pocket), I'd run a steel cable from the bike's grab rail, through a hole in the back of the bag, and then through a locked tab on the case. Last thing I wanted besides actually having to use it was for some lowball to come along, rifle my bag and steal it. Mebbe wave it in my face.

As you may gather, none of this is remotely practical.

After the crackers, I thought screw it. I'll just carry the thing anyway, run the risk of carrying unlawfully, a minor crime, and face the fact that with any routine police pullover—you rolled through that stop sign, your tail light is out—they'll write me up and take my gun. I'll lose in court and some money, and as noted, the gun will remain confiscated until process and bureaucracy run their due course.

Thinking back on it, though, there was one other time I might have thought to go to the Smith. We were at a roadhouse in Minnesota, U.S. 61, a place set back on a little rise across the road from the Mississippi. We stopped for a burger and beer. Down the bar a few stools was a big hefty biker-type guy and a woman, and I nodded to them as we sat down.

We finished first, paid our bill and walked down to the bike. The couple comes out right behind us. This guy is huge. If he appeared hefty in the bar, he did steroids on the way out the door. He's 6'2", probably pushing 300 pounds. He's ruddy-faced, pock-marked, bearded, dirty blond shaggy hair. He's wearing a bandana, T-shirt and a vest. He is one very mean-looking dude.

So is his girlfriend, equally disfavored by nature, nearly as big, and just as ornery in demeanor.

His Harley is parked a few feet away, he walks around and stands next to it, eyes me and the bike up and down, slowly works up a sneer and this look, then lays it on me. It is THE LOOK—the meanest, dirtiest, ugliest look I've ever seen.

It was uglier than the look I got from the softball team the night when I swung at an outside 3-2 pitch instead of waiting out the walk, grounding to second and ending the game. It cost us a title.

Uglier than that.

He held it, longer than was leaving me comfortable, then without speaking a word he swung a ham-like leg over the Hog, and with the girlfriend settled down on the back, fired it up and rode away.

I still don't know why he did it, other than in his own strong, silent way to communicate his disapproval of something, quite possibly the Shadow, more likely the Shadow and me. Maybe even Barbi. Were he to have spoken, he would have said, "I hate your phuquing guts."

It's good to have a strong sense of composure, self-discipline and the will to turn the other cheek.

On the other hand, had this cretin chosen to land a roundhouse to the side of my head, knock me off the bike and then kick in my face, my reserve would not work in my favor, would it?

Nor Barbi's, as it might turn out.

It's a fine line, indeed, as to when one may feel mortally threatened and in fact of that, how one might be prompted to act.

14

TRAVELS WITH MOONIE

New Glarus and Environs

2001-2002

Fred and Moonie, '85 Shadow 1100 and his Excelsior-Henderson. Photo by Brett Nicastro.

15

Espirit de Corps

When Moonie came upon me that night in the village of Cashton, an outpost in the heart of the Kickapoo River Valley in western Wisconsin, I was sprawled out on the seat of the Shadow, hands folded across my chest and my boots propped up on the handlebars.

I was asleep.

It was 11 p.m., four hours after I'd started having battery problems on the way back from the Twin Cities to New Glarus. I'd stopped along the way, checked the water level which read dangerously low—criminally so, one might say, for a so-called seasoned rider. I bought distilled water at a gas station, poured some in, shook it up and continued the ride with little hope.

On State 33 east out of La Crosse, it was at the outskirts of Cashton when I knew I was cooked, battery zapping its last. Only the same sort of dumb luck that seems to befall me more often than I deserve enabled *Donner und Blitzen* to putt-zap-putt a few hundred more yards, carrying us into the small parking lot of a mom and pop filling station, the zaps and the putts choking off.

Seven o'clock on a Sunday night in Cashton. Conveniently speaking—no, not at all.

The most notable thing about Cashton is that it is a trading center for the local Amish community, which is large, spreading down and east through the valley, and while they often travel the roads in their horse-drawn buggies in daytime, you rarely see them at night. If I did, what good might it do me? An overnight stay in a hay loft? A bucket of oats for my bike?

Almost nothing is open. There are no local motels. I'm 100 miles from home and I have 15 bucks in my pocket. If I had any credit cards, they were overdrawn, people haggling me over the phone about long neglected debts that some numbskull had incurred.

I had one choice: Moonie.

It was 2002, and whereas I might have a quarter, Moonie was at the cutting edge of technology. He had a cell phone. Mom and Pop's was still open for a couple of hours and they had a pay phone. I found the quarter and called him. It was a flyer. If he doesn't pick up, if he's out for the night, I am screwed.

He picks up. I explain.

Moonie is down in Iowa County, the other side of the Wisconsin River, a little west of where I was and a good 2 ½ hours removed. He's on a ride with the Apparitions (aka "Apps" or "Spooks" as the slang goes), the New Glarus bike club that Moonie sometimes hangs out with. They're on their way back to New Glarus, but still a good 30 miles out.

"Okay," sez the Moon. "Soon as I get back I'll get the pick-up and come get ya."

Wahl, that's a relief.

But now I have a few hours to kill and I'm in Cashton. I'm told there are 10 bars in the town, but on that Sunday night in the summer, only two or three are open, at least within walking distance for this ol' cowboy with a bad-winded hoss. They're a couple blocks away. I leave the bike and walk over. Business is light, a handful of Sunday night hard-liners trying gamely to fight off the next day. The 15 dollars go quick. I head back to the bike, crawl up on the seat and lie back, promptly falling asleep.

When Moonie arrives, it's a hop and a jump. There's a dock on one side of the station, we push the Shadow up there, Moonie backs in with the pick-up, lays down a couple of boards and we roll *D&B* into the bed, lashing her down.

We made it to Richland Center, halfway to home, before bar time, stopped for an early-morning nightcap, and were back in New Glarus by 3 a.m.

That's what I call friendship. Loyalty. That's what I call a pal.

I first met Moonie on a spring morning in May while I was standing in front of the New Glarus post office and he rode up to deposit some mail. There was a roar and a rumble, and here he comes on this…mmm…unusual looking motorcycle, a big one and distinctively styled. It had those flared fenders that two or three years later I would see on the Rune, with the front having a sort of screwy, pinched bird-beak shape to its nose. There also were these overly largish chrome springs, circling the forks, a hint of Harley there. On the whole, it looked vaguely familiar, yet something I couldn't quite place. Then I did.

It was an Excelsior-Henderson, first one I'd ever seen. I recognized it from pictures. There'd been magazine articles about these folks in southern Minnesota who were well into the process of creating a whole new American motorcycle, first one in decades, and to challenge the Harley supremacy, to create a new myth. Here was their creation.

Or creature, if you will.

We got to talking. Moonie liked his bike, said it was great. He'd bought it specifically, he said, because he wanted an American motorcycle, but not a Harley. This was his chance. The bike he bought was a 2000, one of the last off the line. Now it sat grunting, in all its glory, before me.

I told him I rode, too, was new to town. With that, he invited me on a group ride that Saturday, some kind of charity run, meeting at the Eagle Pass Saloon in Monticello, a few miles south. Cool. Hey, see ya there.

That began what I call a great buddy bikeship. It soon evolved into friendship, although if truth be told, you really can't have one without the other. You enjoy each other's company, rarely if ever a down meeting. I mean, if you're going to be down, why take it out on your buddy? That grows into trust, mutual respect, and if you're riding regular with one or two guys, you better learn quick how they ride, and you better be comfortable with them when you do. Of all the stupid things Moonie and I have done together, I can't think of any time he screwed me up on the bikes. Or I him, for that matter.

I was fortunate to meet Moonie when I did because as far as moving fresh to New Glarus, southern Wisconsin, and knowing nobody goes, Moonie knew everybody. Or if not, they knew him, or something about him at least, some slanderous story from his checkered past. He was born and raised there, the son of a farm-equipment dealer who moonlighted as mayor, played high-school football and buckets, horsed around and raised hell. His jump shots had a high arc, his teammates calling them "moonshots," hence the name.

He enlisted in the Marines, served honorably, if not without an occasional black mark, and came home, picking right up where he'd left off, He got a job selling farm implements, went through a few tribulations so many of us seem cursed to encounter, came out of it reasonably sane and by the time I came upon him was living with a dog and a cat in a house trailer a few miles out County W. He invited me for barbeque and beer. We had a great time. We clicked. It was hard not to like him. He was in his element, and happy as a pig at a trough.

So, upon praising this angel, the rest of the tale.

16

Chew On This

It didn't take long, riding with Moonie, before I was introduced to the Apps. They're headquartered west of New Glarus, low rolling hill country at the southeastern edge of the Driftless Area, in a spacious and tidy clubhouse built among trees on a hillock leading down to a well tended little valley.

Like most biker clubs, this one is grounded in dedication and brotherhood, honor and loyalty, if you like.

If you're going to be an App, if they choose to give you a shot, there is a probationary period in which you are regarded as a "prospect." A prospect spends a year or more displaying his enthusiasm and qualifications: mostly along the lines of schlepping for the bro', clean-up duties around the clubhouse and various small acts of humility and homage—shit details, so to speak.

I used to kid Moonie, whom the Apps had sought to recruit as member, encouraging his presence at parties and rides. "Moonie," I'd say, "you'd be a great prospect—even if you don't like people telling you what to do. It would be just like the Marines."

It was at the Apps' annual Labor Day party, three days of fun and music and nothing but fun and music (wahl, okay, there's food to eat and plenty to drink, the sweetish aroma of herb in the air, and you can camp on the grounds in a tent), when I made my debut. It was fairly inauspicious, 'cept for the fact I was wearing my riding vest (or "Ridin' and Fightin' Vest," as I prefer to call it) and that attracted attention.

The vest is old and ratty, as befits its owner, and festooned not so much with yer standard biker-type patches ("Sturgis 1980", "Black Hills 2000", "Don Gnarly's Harley-Davidson—Bent Tool, Nebraska") but with patches and medals and buttons I had acquired over the years and displayed as the stuff of my life. There are some from the Navy, others representing the VFW, NRA, Bucky Badger, Smith & Wesson, "Don't Tread On Me," personal mementos of meaning, one could say. I also have two political buttons: Teddy Roosevelt, and Goldwater for President, 1964.

One of the Navy patches is from my old ship, *Iwo Jima*, and on that a couple of unit medals we earned. I actually earned a third award by myself, the Good Conduct Medal, but like so many former military vets, I am embarrassed to wear it.

The two I do wear are for National Defense, which during the Cold War they used to hand out to everyone, although in our case it bears merit, I think, for it included three months on station in the central Pacific to take part in the nuclear testing, summer of '62, when I gained the distinction of being among the few folks on earth who have ever witnessed the detonation of a hydrogen bomb.

They triggered it in the ionosphere, some three miles overhead, and told us later had it been dropped at bombing level on the West Coast of America, it would have completely leveled Los Angeles County.

However trite it may read, or sound, it was like seeing God. It was so immense, so brilliant in its terrible power, that nothing else that's ever happened to me in my life has been by comparison any big thing.

The second medal, Armed Forces Expeditionary, is for participation in the Cuban Missile Crisis, barely three months after igniting our bomb. We were dispatched from San Diego to the Caribbean as part of a a large convoy loaded with heavy equipment, munitions and Marines, then spent the next month or so cruising back and forth a few miles off Guantanamo Bay, waiting for the world to cash out.

In our case, subject to shore-to-sea missiles the Russkies on the island were manning, my personal part of it likely would have been focused quite close to home—the bridge of the *Iwo*, per chance, where with a set of headphones and a coal-scuttle hemmit I stood my battle station. As an assault ship, loaded with Marines, we were a primary target.

I copped a line from the political lexicon of the era, the "balance of terror," which was commonly cited as the one fine civilized line keeping the nuclear-armed Soviet Union and U.S. from blasting each other into atoms. For me, with a closer, more introspective view, it was "straddling the balance of terror, my 20-year-old arse hanging over the edge."

You could say, all things considered, it was a formative period of my life.

The day after the party, Labor Day, the Apps were cleaning up. I rode out to the clubhouse, a few miles southwest of New Glarus, to observe what I might call "slaying of the wounded," that is, policing the grounds, putting out smoldering camp fires, rousing drunks from the bushes, picking up crap and tidying up all the loose ends. One of the Apps—I call him the Butcher (most respectfully, you must unnerstan') —was roasting pork on a grill. I asked a few questions about how everything went, nosey and intrusive should one be paranoid, and in doing so, new and unknown—an old guy with some cockamamie motorcycle fetish, riding a Honda, fer Chrissake—I aroused his suspicion. The Butcher, who as it turned out had been in the Navy hissef, observed dryly that I was "pretty salty."

He looked at the insignia sewn on my cap, a red circle inside a larger white one, gray oak leaves scalloped and surrounding.

"What's that, the Royal Air Force?"

"It's a Panzer *cockade*, insignia of the German tank corps."

He looked at my vest, giving it the twice-over. "What about the rest of it? All this shit mean something?"

I was being tested, and he was standing purty close to my face.

"No," sez I, "actually I put 'em on there just for phuqueheads like you to ask about."

A dangerous moment. Was it a bluff and a bad one? Had I miscalculated, overshooting my mouth, destined fast for a fist in the teef? Would they de-pants me, eviscerate the Shadow and string me from a tree, left to the taunts of their fellows and auxiliary ladies and perhaps worse, the goddamn mosquitoes?

Naah. The Butcher stood contemplating this for a moment, relaxed, smiled and snorted, and then speared a chunk of meat, handing it to me on a fork. "Want some?" he said.

I had skated.

As time passed, while never quite reaching the point of becoming the tightest of buddies, the Butcher and I went on nodding, not unpleasant acquaintances, sometimes even sharing a friendly grunt.

We'd see the Apps pretty regular. They often went on club rides, occasionally sponsoring a charity run on behalf of this or that, and these were open to the riding public. Now, whereas the Apps riding together are a disciplined bunch, pairing two abreast instead of staggered, rolling through the straights and curves as one thundering unit, the riding public by contrast will get you everything from experienced bikers, friends of the Apps, to a mishmash of not-quite-ready for group ride might-be's who'd be better off riding solo for a couple more years, learning how to do it right.

Moonie and I would always ride near the front, close to those setting the pace, or else we'd take the rear. In that way, were there a spin-out, shunt or some really serious mishap among the scrambling rabble, we'd either be far enough out in front or behind to avoid it. The risk factor of these rides was exacerbated by alcohol, mebbe even the odd controlled substance.

Although some didn't drink, many did, and with the average ride of 120 to 150 miles, there normally would be a half-dozen stopping points, invariably a roadhouse or tavern. After about the third or fourth one, it got crazier. Moonie and I took to peeling off around then, heading home independently and leaving the mob to the tender mercies of its own making.

Not all of these rides involved the Apps. Some of them we just came across and hooked onto.

There was one out of Riley Tavern near Pine Bluff, a memorial ride in honor of a close friend of the group who had passed. There were around 20 of us and a dozen or so, the organizers, all took off like bats, so we shrugged, said what the hell, and took off after them. We paid our respects at the grave, rode some more routes new to me but which I assumed were well known, and by mid-afternoon it was over. In accord with the plan, someone from the bar showed up in Brigham Park, overlooking Blue Mounds, with a pick-up truck full of beer, soda and snacks. We all gathered round for some fellowship.

Moonie opened a saddle bag, pulled out a big hunk of sausage and began slicing it up with a knife. He walked over to the group, passed some around, and to a man they approved of it hardily.

"Venison, huh?" said one. "This is delicious."

Wahl, eat it right up, I am thinking, so far, so good.

Moonie had shot the deer a few months before, only 10 or 12 miles from where it now was being eaten. This happened to be during the initial outbreak of CWD, Chronic Wasting Disease, which had somehow migrated from whitetails and elk in Colorado and Wyoming to a small section of southwestern Wisconsin, and shown signs of spreading infection, perhaps even depleting the herd. 'Course, on the average there are between 1.3 million and 1.7 million of the critters roaming the state in any one year, banging into cars and motorcycles, so a mild depletion from any cause might not be a bad thing for all. Still, the Department of Natural Resources was alarmed, nearly panicked, and hunters were widely advised to take caution. What if the disease spread to cattle? And so on.

Main problem is, and this remains largely theoretical, that at the root of the disease is something called a *prion*, a "protein in misfolded form" by definition, and otherwise an intrusive and deadly microbiotic agent, highly resistant to neutralization except destruction by the only form known—incinerating it at the extremist of temperatures.

Left thriving, untended in the deer and eaten by humans, it may or may not work its way into the brain of anyone who digests a piece of infected meat. The speculative result is that the diner goes stark raving mad, a babbling and pathetic sub-human, wracked in pain so unbearable that it drives them screaming through the streets before dying a horrible death. Bambi *cum* Zombie, so to speak.

Where Moonie shot the deer, near Arena, was dead phuquing center of the CWD zone.

Riding away, I asked if he wasn't concerned over the origin and health of his kill, whether the guys back at the park would have scarfed so hungrily had they been informed.

"Phuque 'em," he sez, "I eat it."

"Besides, you think I don't know a diseased deer when I kill it?"

He had me there, should I ever have doubted, and Moonie lives to this day.

17

The X Factor

We had some great rides that summer. Moonie's schedule was flexible, I was unemployed. We'd roll through the hills of the Driftless Area. Moonie showing me places I'd bypassed before, never knew they were there. I led him up around Lake Wisconsin and the Baraboo Hills, out to the Mississippi and Prairie du Chien. We roamed wild and free.

Moonie's Excelsior-Henderson was a powerful brute. Highway speed, few limits, and were it not for Smokey, higher insurance, losing yer license, he'd dust me arse. On the twisties, though, the back roads in Green, La Fayette, Iowa, Sauk and Grant counties, it was Freddie to the fore, nod to me. The Shadow has a long third gear, you can hang there all day at 55 mph, 3000 rpm, then punch it up to 75, 85 before the engine starts to scream.

This gave me the tactical advantage of going into curves harder, tapping the brakes, letting the engine brake most of it, holding the line, then accelerating without shifting, copping an edge. On the next straight, he'd catch up, but given the realities of county roads engineered for 45-50 mph speed limits, there aren't all that many of those around.

We came in one day after a typical ass-whuppin'.

"I dunno," sez Moonie, looking at the Shadow askance, "maybe that's just a really fast bike."

Part of his problem, of course, is that he's a big man and I'm not. Moonie goes around 6'2", 210, if he's anywhere near in shape, and I'm 5'9", 155. The Shadow weighs maybe 200 pounds less than his X. I wouldn't necessarily call it skill, either. Fact is, *D&B* is a fast bike.

On top of that were the Henderson's quirks, shortcomings if one must be frank, pains-in-the-ass and expensive to rectify if you happened to have bought one of the gems. It was as though the designers borrowed a line from Shakespeare, Richard III, "sent before [its] time into this breathing world scarce half made up," and conjured it into form.

Headquartered in Belle Plaine, Minnesota, the X people reasoned that with the cruiser market glutted with Harleys, typically expensive and still under huge demand, it might be as good a time as any to offer an alternative—American bike, a bruiser, for people who didn't want Harleys but didn't want Japanese cruisers, either.

They raised a good deal of money, $100 million, some from private investors, and guaranteed loans both local and state. They proceeded to spend a bunch of it on factory and offices, fair enough, but the lavishness of the place—the "Taj McGarage," locals called it—was thought by some to be a little much.

Moreover, on top of this outlay and the subsequent rush to produce something that might turn into profit and dividends sooner than later, they began to feel increasing pressure to roll out a product and get it on the market; here it comes, ready or not. In my estimation, hindsight golden, it hit the showrooms, oh, probably a good year, maybe two before they had it firmly nailed down.

In essence, what they were putting out was a prototype, an innovatively inspired machine that given more development may indeed have met their objectives and dreams. Flawed as it was, however, and with the production line geared up on a schedule to manufacture 20,000 units within the first two years, they ran out of money after only 2,000 were made and the whole operation went rubber side up. In the meantime, the bikes they had sold were starting to break down and folks were complaining. As early as fall of '99, the National Highway Safety Administration had posted a recall.

In Moonie's case, riding his Super X, he got one good riding season out of it before the gears hit the fan and after that the glitches came fast. Among the defects he had over the next two years: three stators replaced, new front wheel bearings, a complete rebuild for the transmission, motor mounts replaced twice, two oil pressure sending units, and a new air cleaner rocker cover. Adding his own hand to the mix (or through God's merciless intervention, perhaps), he installed an oil-cooling unit, hit a rock one day that pierced the reservoir, lost all of the oil and the engine seized up.

Worse yet, by the time all this started happening, the company had already gone under, so there was no warranty to be honored, barely any mechanics who were familiar with such exotica, so every time a repair was undertaken, Moonie would have to break the bike down where it hurt, pull the bad parts, then ship them to California for work by one of the few Xperts on the planet, the "X-Man," they call him. He would rebuild, ship it all back, and Moonie would cobble it together again.

He got pretty good at it, he says. In the process, however, he dropped another 11 grand on top of the $13,900 he paid for it originally. Those are his calculations.

A couple of years after they went bust, the ex-Henderson people hosted a rally in Jordan, Minnesota,. By that time, having moved to Minnesota after leaving New Glarus, I was living with Barbi not far from there, around 35 miles as the freeways merge. Moonie drove up here on a Friday afternoon, in his Jeep with a trailer hauling the X. He stayed overnight, caused the cats consternation, and left early in the morning, riding the bike.

About 11 a.m.—oh, give him a break, it may have been 1 p.m.—I get a call. It's Moonie, telling me the X has broken down at the rally. He's got a tow to a nearby garage where an ex-X factory mechanic has set up a shop to try and keep these things rolling, but he needs a ride back.

"Yer shittin' me," I said.

Then I remember his kindness at Cashton, a veritable prince.

I ride down there on *D&B*, pick him up and we come back.

We're cruising along, north on 169, me at the helm and Moonie riding bitch. I mean, if the Apps had seen it, we would have undergone the grossest and cruelest of jibes. A blessing for us that they didn't, and except for the occasional smart-assed little creep in the backseat of his parents' van, rolling down the window to stick out his tongue and call us fairies, something best kept to ourselves.

A friend of Moonie's from Dodgeville had come to the rally, too. He also trailered his bike, an X nearly identical to Moonie's.

"Why didn't you ask Denny to bring you back?" I asked.

"He broke down, too," sez Moonie, not shitting me.

But hey, I'm not here to trash what arguably may have been a potentially great motorcycle. And from what I understand, had it achieved the vision, it might well have been a great bike after all. All I'm saying is that Moonie got stung. And in a way—how I do love irony—it's an American story, going around/ coming around, circling, arriving often in the same relative place. After ditching the X, Moonie bought an old Harley 1200, had it rebuilt, some nice custom stuff, and painted a bright yellow. It was a hot rod, for sure, but frame-wise, not a very big bike, Not for Moonie, anyway. He'd get on it and all I could think of was an ape on a pony.

His next bike was a Gold Wing, '85 I think. He had the usual problem with the stator, but on the whole it ran all right. Finally, he found a Harley Electra Glide that he was riding over the summer, last time we met.

Ten years later, he's got a fairly reliable American bike and it's paid for, few problems. That's progress.

But I'll still run him through the twisties on the Shadow, and given an absence of state coppers on—an interstate, highly unlikely—*Brunhilde* and I will whup his arse going flat out.

Never happen. We'd both wind up in jail.

18

RIDES OF THE VALKYRIE

Central Minnesota, Points West and East

2002-Present

Fred and his Valk in the Town of Dunn. Photo by Tom Kinney.

19

The Boulder Run

It started out well enough, then soon turned poorly.

Pulled out of Plymouth at 5 a.m. Monday with *Brunhilde*, the '99 Valk Interstate Tourer, loaded to the gills with accouterment appropriate for the venture. The rain suit, for example, which I donned before departure, figuring "What the hell, I might as well put it on now because chances are I'm going to need it." Ran into the first of the rain 60 miles south of the Twin Cities and it continued all the way to south of Sheldon, Iowa. Riding in the rain is feasible, but never a pleasant experience. For one thing, I don't like getting the bike dirty.

But that wasn't the worst part.

With the rain falling hard, I pulled into a truck stop in north Mankato for a cup of coffee and a brief respite, and right behind me came a couple of Harley riders, also from the Cities, who were headed to Wyoming. We chatted for a bit, then decided I'd ride along with them. While they were putting on their rain suits, I went inside for a stop in the head. Got back out and off we went. We were 20 miles south when I reached for something in my fanny pack when "Whoa!" there was no fanny pack there!

Damn, I'm thinking; I must have left the sumbitch in the head.

With that, nary so much as a wave goodbye to the Harley riders, I turned around and backtracked. Pulled into the truck stop again, headed willy-nilly to the head, and the worst of my fears were realized. No fanny pack lying on the floor or hanging on a hook in the stall.

Damn again! Some sumbitch musta came in and found it, claimed it for his own. Either that, or mebbe a Samaritan had picked it up and turned it in. I asked the clerks at the counter. Nope, sorry old fella, no fanny pack here.

Now, a fanny pack is a fanny pack, although this is one that I've had for years and to which I have become quite attached. It's leather, the front covered with fringe, three zip pockets and a hidden, pull-away pocket in the back that is just the right size for, say, a Smith & Wesson J-Frame revolver, stainless steel, three-inch barrel and chambered in .357 Magnum.

The good news here, as it were, is that the gun wasn't in the fanny pack. Although I have a concealed-carry permit for Minnesota, it is not recognized as valid in Iowa, Nebraska or Colorado, the three states I'd be riding through. So the gun, cased and unloaded, good citizen that Iyam, was still secure in the trunk of the Valk.

What I was losing in the pack, however, were two speed-loaders and 10 rounds of 125 grain, hollow-point .357, an iPod Nano loaded with most of my music, a cell phone that I'd only owned for a week and had barely learned how to use, a few odds and ends, and worst of all—my totem bag.

The totem bag, a little deerskin pouch filled with icons I'd scrounged to represent the Four Elements, I've had since the early '80s. I "consecrated" it one morning at dawn on the banks of the upper Hudson River in the Adirondack Mountains of upstate New York. I've carried it on all my travels—consider it "lucky"—a totem, if you will.

Wahl, that was that, I thought, and got on a pay phone to call Barbi back in the Cities to see if she could get in touch with the phone company, cancel my new phone in case somebody tried to use it, and order me a new one that with any kind of luck could be mailed ahead to Boulder by the time I got there. They could, she said, and after sitting there over another cup of coffee for a while, pissing and moaning over my loss, I climbed back onto *Brunhilde* and proceeded south again through the rain.

Weather lifted by the time I reached Sioux City, and Monday afternoon in eastern Nebraska was nearly perfect...were it not for the flooding. The Platte River Valley was full after a week of rain, the creeks overflowing, and my plan to diagonal from Sioux City to Grand Island was thwarted by a detour. The detour then was detoured and only by luck did I find myself coming out of the maze in a place I could find on my map—Elkhorn, just above Lincoln. That was nearly 12 hours into the epoch, some 475 miles, so I decided to call it a night and lay over at a motel.

It was a truck-stop motel, cheap but offering free phone service, so I put up my 39 bucks, found my room and settled in to the sounds of a group hanging around outside on the stairs and veranda who I presumed to be, mmm, weekly tenants. The clank of castaway empties, cackles and "mutha phuques" lasted well after midnight.

I took advantage of the free phone, called Barbi and she asked about the motel.

"You wouldn't like it," I said. "Think of it this way—I wore flip-flops into the tub for my shower."

Morning broke both warm and clear in Lincoln, but by 6:30, 20 miles west on I-80, I encountered a heavy wall of low pressure and fog so thick that it condensed on my windshield and began to bead like it would were I riding in rain. This went on for 40-50 miles, during which often I couldn't see anything beyond the tail lights of the car or truck in front of me. It was damp, cool, and oddly, there was a crosswind at work that heightened the chill. It was enough to have me pause at a wayside, dig into the right-side hard bag and pull out a set of my heavy leathers that I'd packed only for such eventuality.

At Kearney, where I-80 takes a turn to the north and North Platte before dipping southwest again, I dropped down south 20 miles to U.S. 34, which runs east-west just above the Kansas border.

Ah, how refreshing. Two lanes, old but well-paved, this baby runs straight as an Arapaho arrow from Holdrege, Nebraska, to Fort Morgan, Colorado, some 300 miles up and down roller-coaster hills, surprisingly mindful of the southern sector of Wisconsin's Driftless Area, and virtually, or practically so, without much human intervention.

Oh, yeah, there was the occasional pick-up or semi, the usual locals heading here and there, but otherwise virtually phuquing nobody—and not in the least any sheriffs. Better yet, most of the time, because of the topography, I could see so much as a good mile ahead of me. I mean everything. Traffic coming toward me, traffic behind me (such as it was), crossroads, even at one point a prairie dog, fer Chrissake. This, with the state speed limit set at a brisk 65 mph, allowed me to cruise at mebbe 70 legally, but as much as 80, 90 and even 110 without much of any sort of problem.

The 110, I only hit once, just for the hell of it; the 90 on two or three passing situations; but the 80 mph, for much of the stretch, purty much *de rigueur.*

I tell you, there's nothing quite like a 1520cc, 94-horsepower, six-cylinder engine banging along for miles at a time at 4000 rpm and 80 miles per hour. Music to me ears, food for the soul of a biker, even though I was wearing my helmet, which muffled a tad the Cobra Six-Pack exhausts.

I've never experienced it before, being able to go anywhere on a bike or in a car, that fast for so long at a stretch, without worrying particularly about either traffic or gendarme.

It's the best testimony I could ever make to oft-stated claim—the Valk Interstate arguably is the greatest highway cruiser ever made.

I pulled into Boulder around 6:30 p.m., CDT, or 5:30 Mountain Time, picking up an hour on the way. Essentially, 12 hours in the saddle, given stops around every hour or so for a short rest and stretch, hydration, gas, and as I found along the way, caffeine and cannabis for a nicely balanced little pick-me-up.

Boulder is pretty, at the "foothills" of the Rocky Mountains. The foothills are actually mountains, were they situated anywhere else in the country, and it's chock-full of young and healthy-looking people on bicycles, runners and joggers, and attractive stay-at-home moms pushing baby strollers along quiet, narrow streets and tree-shaded walkways when they're not staying home. Once upon a time, we may have called them Yuppies.

Everybody has a dog—that, and a couple of plastic water bottles they carry around. Correctly, most of the owners are quite diligent about cleaning up after them, so with the water bottles carefully discarded in the trash cans, there is little refuse around. About all I saw was an occasional cigarette butt—and almost all of those were mine.

The week with my son and his family was wonderful. There was a 2½-year-old grandson, Sam, and he and his dad and I spent Father's Day together.

Righteous.

20

High Plains Drifter

I headed toward home Monday morning, riding east from Cheyenne on I-80 into Nebraska, then took U.S. 71 north through Scottsbluff all the way to Hot Springs, South Dakota. It was a road almost identical to U.S. 34, straight, up and down, so again I made good time.

Got to the Black Hills around 5, went partway through Custer National Park before cutting over to U.S. 385 and on up to Deadwood. Nearly lost *Brunhilde* once or twice in the park on a tight and curvy gravel road, even at the posted 15 miles per hour; had to brake in the middle of the mess for a deer, then sit and wait a few minutes for your obligatory bison herd to cross leisurely from one wallow to another.

Stayed in Deadwood overnight, a guest of the, er, "Hickok House."

If it weren't for Wild Bill Hickok dying there, I believe the Sioux might still have it—along with the honky-tonks and gambling parlors, which for yer average passer-through is about all there is. It's a rustic and pretty place, though, way down in the V of a deep gulch flanked by high and steep Black Hills, which because of the fact that the sun takes a powder early in the afternoon, truly look black. On the downside, cell phone signals run to shit.

Yeah, I had another cell phone—mailed to me in Boulder by the company—so at least this time on the road, I was no longer incommunicado.

Rode east through Sturgis in the morning, north on State 73 to Newell and then east again on U.S. 212.

Damn, there's a third road out there that's straight as a stick and camel-backed, high and low, that on the high sides gives you great visibility. Again, no traffic; again I flew, noodling along at 110 again twice, and again, simply for the hell of it.

It was sort of like Bill Clinton, years after the Lewinsky affair, when he was asked by an interviewer, "Why did you do it?"

"Because I could," Bubba said.

There were mishaps, a couple close ones, all in the spacious midst of the Great High Plains.

One guy was diddling along at around 10, 15 mph as I came upon him while descending a hill and dropped to third gear. No turn signal. What the hell?

So I start to go around him slowly and bigger than shit he starts to turn left down a long dirt side road—with his signal on now—doofus!—which was a tad late for me. I managed to brake enough to slow *Brunhilde* down a car's length short of the target, then had to wrestle her thousand-pound load to a reasonably controlled stop. That is, I didn't tip over.

I nearly ran out of gas on the Cheyenne River reservation. It's solely a Sioux enclave, I found out later, nothing to do with the Cheyenne except for the name of shallow, languishing river passing through that I crossed at some point. I mean, talk about the middle of nowhere. It's a long, long stretch, and if you don't fill up at the mom and pop station in Eagle Butte…wahl, then you're as dumb as me.

Making it worse, I could have got gas, but instead stopped in only for a coffee and a cigarette. There were a few of the tribe hanging around out in front, and though most of them paid no attention, I did catch one fella peering at me narrowly as I walked back to the bike.

Then it dawned on me. I was wearing my Ridin' and Fightin' vest, and on the back in the center is an embroidered Thunder Bird patch, fortunately for me, perhaps, made in fact by the Sioux. Only difference is that this one happened to be made not at Cheyenne River, but by a native craftsman at Pine Ridge, a couple of hundred miles south. Being both of the Lakota Nation, I trusted they weren't in bad stead, nor should a sacred symbol worn by one or the other have cause to offend. A white eyes, however; wahl, that could be a different story. But I went on my way unmolested, thanking the Great Spirit fervently that it hadn't been made by a Crow or Pawnee. Bad medicine, that.

Miles and miles later, I was down to reserve when I finally found a Sinclair, pulled in and pumped 6.3 gallons into my 6.9-gallon tank. Fuel to spare, but not all that much when you're in the middle of the Great Middle.

A word to the wise. You take a long trip, even with a huge gas tank, and you have enough room for a plastic jug, gallon and a quarter, take it along, just in case. Dumb me for not doing that.

Some 20 miles east of Gettysburg, I came upon a long stretch of heavy gravel—24 miles of it, according to a sign I'd passed, one which encouraged motorists to consider taking an alternate route.

Hmm, to where? Mobridge? Pierre? San Antonio?

I sat there for a minute, gazing ahead at what I knew I'd be in for, and then, willing to explore a calculated challenge, decided to try and take a crack at it, anyway. I eased on in, immediately found myself nearly up to the foot pegs in chunks the size of golf balls and quickly relented. Following furrows, speaking to *Brunhilde* imploringly ("C'mon, baby—you can make it") I managed to bring her to a stop without falling over, wrestled her around in the middle of the road and beat a slow retreat.

At a bar in a hamlet called Orient, hauling out my map, a couple of friendly old gents and the bartender showed me a couple of county roads to the south and northeast that would lead me back out.

It was 10 p.m. or so by the time I got to Watertown. They had the radar on at the Stop 'n' Rob and there was holy hell in the way of storms and tornados being played out in northeastern Nebraska and northwestern Iowa. I was just above it. Fresh full of caffeine and boo, I decided to push on. Got to Montevideo, Minnesota, around midnight, cut northeast up a state road to U.S. 12 and Willmar, and followed that on home.

The sky from Monte all the way east was lighting up like a campfire at the Boy Scouts big rally at Valley Forge, all around, the entire horizon. There was a pale moon smoked by wisps of clouds, and through one woodsy stretch near Granite City, I felt for a while like Ichabod Crane. Pulled the next 60 miles and into the driveway at 2:05 a.m., splatters of rain on my head.

It was 613 miles in 16 hours. Figuring I stopped for 10 to 20 minutes out of every 60, thereabouts, I still averaged 60 mph, Deadwood to Plymouth.

The Valk performed heroically. Aside from having to handle it on the gravel or push it around a parking lot, find the right angle to park at a curb so it's not slanting so hard to port that I'll never get it back up without help, it's the greatest all-around bike I've ever ridden and designed damn near perfectly for the purpose for which it is mainly intended.

But I've said that before. Stop me if I say it again.

Standing in the garage, lightning in the sky, thunder overhead, rain now coming down in yer literal deluge, I lit up a smoke and leaned against Barbi's car. I looked around, giving the once-over to *Donner und Blitzen,* parked where I'd left it 10 days before. There was something slung over the saddle.

It was my fanny pack, leather and fringe, still packed with all the stuff I'd put in there on the day that I left.

What a dumb ass.

I zipped it open, took out all the stuff including, by the way, my sacred totem bag.

Lucky fer me.

21

In Quest of a Queen

The first time I saw a Valkyrie Interstate in the flesh, I was shocked and amazed.

It was on a group ride west of the Twin Cities in 2001. The bike was introduced in '99, I'd seen a picture in a moto magazine and was impressed. Huge, was my first thought, but nowhere near as much as when I actually saw one. It was sitting in a roadhouse parking lot, another 100 bikes clustered around, but this one, painted metallic purple, stood out like a small truck. I approached it from behind, marveling at the width—the trunk, Flat Six engine, airflow pods, giant gas tank and fairing. How could anyone possibly handle this thing? The owner came by and I asked.

"Great," he said. "No different than any bike; compared to most, even better."

Wahl, as I was to learn, he was correct in theory but hedging a bit in the fine print.

Yes, it handles remarkably well on the road, even five feet away from a curb, but getting there, especially if you're not a large man, can be a problem. Everyone who has ever owned one admits this. The dry weight, according to factory specs, is 774 pounds. You fill up the 6.9-gallon gas tank and you're adding another 42. That's a real load to be pushing around, say, backing up to a curb, or if you're coming to a stop and carrying a passenger—even a small one. I weigh 155, Barbi is a smidgen over 100. Pile on another 20 to 40 pounds of travel gear, and you're looking at something better than 1,100 pounds. Even the idea is intimidating.

There came a time, however, around '04, when I decided that I wanted to ride longer; that is, 300 miles in a day or more without crippling myself or a passenger. That meant I had to move beyond the Shadow for something that holds the road, especially an interstate, regardless of most every condition, provides more comfort, an amenity or three, greater distance per tank, increased luggage space, but something that will still roar like a lion and cruise damn near forever at top highway speeds without flinching. Oh, yeah—and have some spare oomph in the bowels for that ever welcome jump in tight situations.

Briefly, I thought about a Harley. If there was any one thing that caused hesitation in getting a Valk, it was the size. Fact is, however, give or take 100 pounds, a Harley dresser is nearly as large. They just don't quite look that way, and I imagine that's mostly because of their V-Twin engines, vis-à-vis the Flat Six, smaller gas tanks and a wheelbase that's around three inches shorter than the Valk's.

Then again, everyone has a Harley, or so it seems, anyway—so much that after the big marketing boom in the '90s, everyone who wanted one had one. Conversely, not many have Valk Interstate Tourers, and in retrospect even most early critics admit today it is the most powerful cruiser on the highway.

Fact is, though, compared with anything smaller, there are relatively few big cruisers today. Honda chose to make them for only two years, '99-'01. They continued making a standard model (no frills) and tourer (no trunk, no fairing, smaller gas tank) for a year after that, then for reasons all but unfathomable to anyone other than Honda executives (most of them now deposed, one would hope), tried to change over most everything that defined the Valk concept, a five-year run, '97 to '02, by introducing the Rune.

In creating it, Honda's rationale was to make something super—not unlike the Excelsior Henderson experiment—the next generation of motorcycles. Compared to most everything else in the cruiser world, it was two steps ahead. It was state-of-the-art with innovative technical features, minute attention to detail and a body finish that equaled if not even surpassed the resident champion Harley's.

It was born of a string of concept bikes Honda was developing in the '90s, the T-series. They were Valkyrie-based but radically remodeled to create what came to be called a "neo-retro" effect. Others said it was a "'50's-styled hot rod married to a rocket."

They used the same basic engine found in the Valk and the pre-2000 Gold Wings, but jacked it up to 1800cc. That's fair enough, for around the same time Suzuki was developing its Boulevard and Yamaha its Road- and Stratoliner series, 1800s as well. The question remained as to how many cruiser-type riders needed that big an engine, that much power, even wanted it, but there was a small market there as the Zooks and Yammies eventually proved. Where the Rune went wrong was on two other salient points.

The design showed sort of a hump-de-hump-de-hump profile, smoothly achieved far as humps go, but in my estimation screwed up royally by a couple of big, fat, flared fenders that hung low over the wheels, especially the rear, which to the designers' misfortune resembled an elephant's ass.

That, and they tacked on a hooded headlight that stuck way out in front, extending the profile something akin to the old Western Union logo, Mercury in his winged hemmit, reaching for the sun. It was just a little much, more than that to be frank. Same might be said for the wheelbase, 68.9 inches, more than three inches longer than the Valk Interstate, which if you're keeping score is nearly six feet long. And like the Valk's, discounted by some critics for the weight, it was more than 800 pounds.

But here's the real killer—the price. Whereas the Suzuki and Yamaha were selling for a reasonable $15,000 or so, the sticker price on the Rune was $25,000-plus. That's top-end Harley country. And if you were to tack on chrome wheels and another doodad or two, you were looking at 30 grand.

It was not well received. Nobody bought it. Today some collectors might pay $14,000 for this bird, an American icon, an exceptional machine on the drawing board but fated to be ranked with the Edsel as to how it might be remembered. As early as '06 you could buy an '03 or '04 off a dealer's floor, six zeroes on the odometer, for as little as 5,000 bucks.

They produced it for only three years, '03 and '04 and slouching into '05 then shut it down. By that time, with the money they'd pissed away in new factory machinery, there was no way they were going to retool, leastwise for reproducing anything close to the original Valkyrie line.

A terrible mistake had been made, Honda was stuck in a trap of its own making, and although a few would remain, The Ride of the Valkyries as we knew it was doomed—a *fait accompli*.

But in my case, this was 2004 and the saga was still unfolding. The ill-fated Rune, fresh on the market but quickly destined for the dust bin of motorcycle history, was not even so much as a gleam in my eye. I thought it was ugly and way overpriced. The older Valks, the whole line, were well tested and ready, and I wanted one badly.

By the time this quest began, I'd been living for a couple of years in the Twin Cities—a west 'burb, actually, about two miles east of where the sticks begin (or moreover the Plains, which is largely the prevailing condition in Minnesota unless you are near to the bluffs along the Mississippi River or in the north, which is predominantly lakes and tall trees).

I'd left New Glarus, which I'd come to love dearly, over a dispute with an employer. He hadn't met our business agreement, much as I understood, and I had grown progressively anxious, antsy and petulant, neglecting some of my responsibilities as matters ground on, mostly out of spite. One night I got a bellyful of Stoli and called him at home at 9 p.m., told him what I thought of his operation.

Heh.

Now, New Glarus, Wisconsin, is not exactly the spot for a guy in his '60s, recently divorced (Mar and I, married 19 years, had gone our ways) and with no discernible assets beyond a dying cat, a couple of guns and a 15-year-old motorcycle. Figuratively and literally, I was not making any money there.

I had been dating Barbi, an old and dear friend who had also divorced, and she lived in the Twin Cities. Along with our growing relationship, she eventually helped convince me that we might prosper better together there. In New Glarus, the alternative was hanging around the Sportsman's Bar or Puempel's Olde Tavern, waiting for a response to that application I'd made to an ad in the paper by an Angus beef breeder who was seeking an "ex-journalist and jack-of-few trades with a working knowledge of cow insemination." In the Cities, said Barbi, I might expand my horizons.

As noted, this was true, but largely to the degree of topography only—the "big skies" that begin about 60 miles west of the Mississippi and St. Croix rivers and another 30 miles west of our home at the eastern edge of what I've come to call Minnesota's "ranch country," low rolling hills prevalent with horse farms and reminiscent somewhat of areas in Wisconsin west of Madison that I'd learned to regard so fondly. Beyond that, the terrain flattens prodigiously.

For a newcomer, accustomed to pronounced topographical variation, it is difficult if not next to impossible to discern whether one is in Minnesota or any of the five states (Wisconsin discounted) nearby. This first became starkly evident on one of our earliest rides through the wheat and cornfields.

We'd gone west 60 miles on the Shadow, then dropped south another 75 to visit New Ulm, the predominantly Germanized, formerly immigrant community in the Minnesota River Valley west of Mankato. For mile upon mile upon mile, we followed straight roads with nary a bend or a rise, not even so such much as a hillock, all surrounded as far as the eye could see by row upon row of cornfields and yer amber waves of grain. I remarked on it, sarcastically, but eventually started to appreciate the setting, if for nothing else, the setting itself. "You know," I said, "if you were to grow up here, perhaps never leave, I'm sure that you'd think this is beautiful." Barbi concurred.

Then I spoiled it.

"Of course, if you were to grow up in, say, Saudi Arabia, I'm sure you'd feel the same way about the rocks and the sand."

The newcomer was adapting grudgingly. But if I was to enjoy to its fullest extent the endless bounty of this fruited plain, it was going to have to be on a larger and more comfortable motorcycle.

22

Brunhilde

I found the Valk on Carsoup. It was out in Fergus Falls, damn near all the way to Fargo, and I rode the Shadow out there to give it a look. It was a beauty, for sure. Had only 17,278 miles, barely broken in. The guy who was selling, second owner, had bought it principally for one ride, to the Rockies with a bunch of Harley buds, and after that he bought a motor home and he and the wife didn't have much time for the bike what with going off to weekend country-western music fairs, that sort of stuff.

I gave it a test ride, more or less. I rode it out of his driveway, second time I'd ever been on one of the beasts, and managed to make it down a gravel road and out to the county highway. I took it up the road a few miles, got it turned around slowly at a crossroad, and then rode it back. It was big, as I'd known, too big actually, but by the end of the test I had talked myself into the idea I could ride it. I wanted that bike.

We dickered a bit over the price. He was adamant, and as he pointed out, this little baby was still almost new and had everything on it, chrome candy, Küryakyn pegs, Cobra pipes and a satellite radio hook-up. I asked if he could hold it a week, not sell it out from under me to somebody else.

"Hey," he said, "anybody who'd ride all the way here from Minneapolis just to see it, I'm giving you the edge."

The next week, Barbi and I drove out to get it. The owner had ridden it to town, parked it in front of a bank. I lopped my leg over the saddle, turned it on and off we went. All I was missing was Fiscus.

"Ready for the Arboretum?" he'd said.

Riding back on State 55, I was extremely cautious. The air in the tires was low, so I pumped them up, but that was the least of my problems. The seat was too high, the handlebars set too wide, too far forward and low, and every time I came to a stop, I would lurch forward, the great front-end weight heaving me forth. A good handful of front brake would have helped, that and a good firm step on the rear, but I was used to feathering the brake on the Shadow, and the difference of 300 pounds proved that if I was really serious about stopping this hulk, that didn't mean treating it soft.

About 50 miles out of Fergus, I pulled into a convenience station to slurp down a Coke. Barbi, trailing behind in the car, pulled in behind me.

"At this rate," she said, "we're never going to get to Minneapolis. Are you sure you can ride this thing?"

I grunted, but held my peace.

State 55 is a two-lane highway and as most of those roads go, there's not often much room to pass. Spurred on by Barbi, however, bearing down on me arse, I came upon opportunities, a couple of trucks and a motor home. Each time I passed, only nudging the throttle, I was astounded to see the speedometer jump to 80, even 90 mph. And I mean, that was only a little bit of crank.

Oh boy, I was thinking. What great phuquing potential.

Now, all I had to do was learn to ride it.

It was only a day later I almost dumped it. We were candy-assing along a few miles from home, I went up a residential street to turn it around, and at a three-way stop figured I had enough room to do it slick, same as I would with the Shadow. Ho-ho, not so fast, Mac. The length of the thing was not made for yer average intersection. On top of that, we were in some gravel, and it was only by getting my feet down and posting a Herculean effort that I avoided a fall. This time, Barbi held her piece, but I knew what she was thinking. I was thinking the same thing.

Maybe the funniest time was a couple of weeks later. We went out on a regional ride, Fred poking along in subservient homage to the mass of the monster, and when we got back home I asked for an assessment. I thought I was doing a little better.

"When are you going to start riding it like the Shadow?" she asked.

I counted to 10, silently, then handed her the keys. "Here," I said, "you try riding the sumbitch."

The last two months of the summer went on the same way. One time we decided to investigate Lake Maria State Park, a little way southeast of St. Cloud. The first two blocks of the narrow road leading in was paved, then it turned to dirt, rutted, and the night before it had rained. I labored it through to the lake, nearly taking a dive when confronted by a car coming our way, and after we'd surveyed the lake, Barbi asked if we could make it back out again.

"That, or we're gonna stay here," I said.

Another time we were down in Excelsior, stopping off at a lakeside joint on Minnetonka that caters mostly to boaters and swells, but bikers not excluded. We were coming out of the parking lot across the street, the exit was narrow and from where we were, angled and up a small rise. There was two-way traffic on the street, and at the top of the rise I'd have to stop on the sidewalk and look both ways before pulling out. To make the angle, I'd have to turn the front wheel, not keep it straight, which at slow speeds on any motorcycle can leave you susceptible. I didn't do it quite right.

Fortunately, there was a grassy slope next to us and rather than flop on concrete, we rather slowly tipped over onto it, the Valk resting precisely on the right engine guard, which is part of the reason it's there. We got out from under it, no harm done, and between the two of us, me under the handlebars and Barbi grabbing hold of a bag rack and giving a nudge with her arse, we got it back up.

This was encouraging. Hitherto, I figured I'd need a block and tackle or a crane to pull it off.

It took me until the next season before I finally got a reasonable hold on it. The main reason was two modifications I made—handlebar risers, which brought the bars up and back toward me a couple of inches, and a different seat. It had come with an aftermarket Mustang, not a bad seat at all, but for my inseam about two inches high. The replacement, an "Ultimate," lowered me considerably, at least to the point where I could flat-foot it at stops; that is, get both feet down flat on the pavement so that I wasn't tippy-toeing it on the balls, thereby securing a tenuous balance that provided a modicum of greater stability. Little by little, I was catching on, wising up.

I dubbed the beast *Brunhilde*—Queen of the Valkyries.

(That's "Broon-hill-deh," by the way.)

23

Old Friends

It was a hot afternoon in July, and we were cooling our heels and throats at the Hog Wild Saloon.

The saloon is in Henderson, a small farming community set on the west bank of the Minnesota River, about halfway south between the Twin Cities and Mankato. Known best for flooding every spring and an annual festival at which they crown a Sauerkraut Queen, Henderson also is a convenient stopover for bikers who cruise up and down river.

There were only a few of us there, but sitting across the room at a table by himself was this one fella looking our way. I recognized him, someone I'd seen a few times up north in Hamel and Corcoran, our neck of the woods, who'd shown at Inn Kahoots, Hamel's most notorious biker/volleyball/softball hangout, and on local group runs. He rides a '90s model-blue Soft Tail if I recollected correctly.

Sizing him up at first glance—short and stocky, leaning toward the husky, shaven head and full mustache—he raises the image of a lieutenant colonel in the NKVD, the Soviet secret service during the Stalin years. Standing up, ambling toward us bear-like in old beat-up brown leathers, he is transformed into a character from *Jeremiah Johnson*—a mountain man, and the guy who comes across a roaming band of Indians while riding with Johnson and surreptitiously transfers an array of scalps he has taken to the unobservant Johnson's saddle horn. If I were to name him, it would be Isaiah or Caleb.

"Name's Joseph," he says, and hands me a paw.

We acknowledge that we've seen each other around. We bring up a few folks we may know in common, places we tend to hang out, and a shared familiarity with the same *petit circuit* favored most by west Metro-based bikers— 60 miles north, 30 miles west and 80 miles south, a strip of fairly scenic territory which then quite abruptly melds with the plains. It's about as much as one can squeeze in conveniently and comfortably on a one-day recreational ride.

We chat a bit more, then he pops a stunner.

"I hear you're from Madison, right?"

"Yes."

"You ever know a guy named Fiscus?"

Boiing!

For a moment, I am speechless.

"*Mike* Fiscus?" I say.

Joseph breaks into an expectant grin, the glint in his eyes hinting of some great inside joke, one of which we both know the punch line.

"Yeah—Mike. You know him?"

"Know him? Mike Fiscus turned me on to bikes."

Forty years earlier, after Joseph left home in the Cities to work on the oil fields in Wyoming, he migrated to Colorado, the little ski towns, for a few months of bumming around. I'd known several guys from Madison who'd done the same, Fiscus being one. He and Joseph met up somewhere—Breckenridge, I think—and started a friendship.

I'd first met Fiscus while in high school, a summer softball league. I knew him as a quick, hard-nosed guy, not big but pound for pound a battler. A standout athlete in track and field, he continued to compete at what was known then as the Wisconsin State University at

Platteville, where when not long-jumping, cutting class or carousing, he studied art, an occupation that became his life's passion. He painted, sculpted and created ornate decorative objects. The Colorado sojourn, I believe, was to gain new experiences and insights through what at the time was a hip artists' haven. Why eventually he returned to Madison, I don't know, but he had long Madison ties.

I had seen Mike only twice over the years since our early moto adventures. Once was not long after his Colorado stay when we met over breakfast at the Café Palms in the Washington Hotel in Madison, downstairs from the offices of the newspaper I was editing. Over coffee, we caught each other up on what we'd been doing; I had been writing, birthing this newspaper, and Mike had been working his art.

If anything struck, it was the deep pool of soul in his eyes, reflective of something I hadn't seen there before. It could have been weariness, even sorrow, but in retrospect I think it was that vague vision of dreams fading, a shadow of doubt, a hovering specter of unrequited fulfillment.

The spark was there, the James Dean demeanor still evident—an inbred defiance of the world and much of its ways that is not uncommon among artists, and the quiet, resigned confidence suggesting that he not only knew the joke but who it was on. There was a shade of unwelcome change—an intrusion of maturity, perhaps—and the creeping recognition that the kind of life he had hoped for just might be in jeopardy, giving ground slowly to time's unsentimental passage, the loss of our youth, and looming mortality.

Under the circumstances, knowing Mike as little as I did, really, but understanding intuitively, it would not have surprised me greatly if I were to learn that he lived out the rest of his life in quiet dissipation.

"So, where is he now?" I asked Joseph.

He wasn't sure, nor was I, but my hunch was it had to be Madison. Going our ways, Joseph and I agreed that one of these days we ought to ride down and surprise him.

That led to the next month of intermittently riding with Joseph. I was still very much into working my way into finding myself on the Valkyrie, this "Hondapotamus" as some owners had taken to calling it. I was yet to make any of the modifications that would settle things later, so learning to maintain balance, which is basic, the focal point of controlling all that power and weight, was an ongoing test.

I was nowhere near comfortable. If there was anything at all that was encouraging, it's that I'd only dumped it once. Gently. My ride to Henderson with Barbi that day was among the first since we'd bought it in which my confidence was increasing enough to risk taking it out of the cul-de-sac where we live, or the nearby high school parking lot to practice, and out on the road.

Sure hope nobody gets hurt.

Joseph, a seasoned rider with a swashbuckler's flair, showed a fair bit of the cavalier in his applications. He had a habit of riding too close, side by side, so that if one was not totally comfortable with the proximity, one might become uneasy, if not rattled. Had I been riding the Shadow, it would have troubled me less. But on *Brunhilde*, which had yet to be mastered, it tended to be disconcerting.

Another thing he'd do, although graciously enough only at those times when he was ahead far enough up the road to not throw a close follower into a passing fit of apoplexy, he would reach down periodically to fiddle with something at the side of his bike, lean back to secure a buckle on a saddlebag, and for his most outrageous stunt let go of the handlebars, placating an itch or placing both hands behind his head, scratching, stretching, flexing and relaxing.

One night, he nearly got me twice.

We were at a stop light in Wayzata, County 101 and State 12, headed for dinner at a supper club, the Ox Yoke Inn in Maple Plain. I was to the right in the turning lane, Joseph to my left. Having not been around those parts for all that long and not yet familiar with much of the territory, I nodded to him to show us the way. He did, helter-skelter, promptly making a right turn across my front wheel at the same moment I let out the clutch, leaving me in a desperate grab at the lever to disengage it again, hitting hard on both brakes and wavering for a long instant on boot toes atop my 840-pound behemoth. I recovered, and followed him out Highway 12.

On County 6, nearing our destination, Joseph overshot County 92, as did I trailing him, and with no traffic in sight he did a U-turn. So did I, but not quite so facile as Joseph, managed barely to wrestle *Brunhilde* around in the right direction, turning close to the shoulder, when alongside me roars Joseph, same shoulder, scaring the snot out of me.

When we got to the restaurant, I pointed it out.

"What?" said Joseph, waving his fork in the air.

I looked him over for a moment, deciding at that point that what I see is what I've got.

"O-kay," I said. "You buy the meal."

It was that night we decided we'd drop in on Fiscus.

24

Bringing It All Back Home

We went down on a Saturday. Barbi was out of town, a business trip, and I was left for the weekend to fend for myself. I figured we'd rustle up Mike in Madison, have a few cocktails and yuks, and then ride to New Glarus and stay over at Moonie's.

The first half of the ride was uneventful, the Cities to Black River Falls, angling east on I-90/94 just below Tomah. Joseph took the point, cruising around 75, with me doddering along a few bike lengths back, keeping it down to a couple miles below 70 on a road posted at 65. Had I been riding *Donner und Blitzen*, I likely would have been right on his tail and dicing, one eye cast for Smokey. Still wooing *Brunhilde*, however, I opted for a cautious engagement. Besides, a couple of speeding tickets picked up in previous years aboard *D&B* had left an impression—bad points on my record and higher insurance premiums.

I'm usually pretty savvy about who is behind me, who's coming up fast, who's even back there. As sometimes happens, however, you'll glance in the mirror, see nothing, look back to the road, and suddenly from behind that hillock you just ambled over comes something going so fast you are startled.

It was on a stretch between Camp Douglas and Lyndon Station that the shitstorm nearly hit. I was watching Joseph, who was closing fast on two or three back-markers, solid citizens loafing along around 60, and I expected him to pull out and pass. I'd just checked my mirror. Split seconds later, alongside me comes a super-size touring bus, "Rascal Flatts" on the side, and the driver easily doing 90.

Behind him, front grill to rear bumper, came the first of the equipment trailers—one, two, three, maybe four, and then another line of U-Haul-size trucks, all at the same breakneck speed.

They had themselves yer veritable convoy—good ol' boys from Tennessee, headed to Milwaukee and the Wisconsin State Fair to make their next gig on time after playing the night before in Minneapolis. From my point of view, it was like a freight train, a solid line of screaming steel.

I saw Joseph pull out. He hadn't seen them, but now he did—the convoy so close to his side that one of the yokels could have reached out a window and grabbed hold of his ear. I was already tapping the brakes, gearing down into fourth and third, setting up for the worst. In the next instant, I expected to see an explosion straight out of *Easy Rider* and to spend the next several hours picking up pieces of Joseph across the Monroe County countryside. Maybe some of mine.

But Joseph reacted quickly—very quickly—quite possibly the most critically adroit thing he's ever done in his life. Caught between the back-markers and this train of terror, he stayed on the line.

It's called lane-splitting, a maneuver that in most states is illegal, save for California where you might pull it off should the CHPs not be near, but here, in the tightest of pinches, he rode the striped line between the two lanes, hunkered down in his saddle, withstanding the roar and buffeting rush.

The Rascals, I presumed, made their gig in plenty of time, arriving in Milwaukee, 150 miles east of us, about 10 minutes later.

First stop in Madison was at the Crystal Corner Bar on Willy Street. I needed a drink.

Second stop was the Echo Tap on West Main, a venerable old watering hole for generations, a vestige of Madison's hardscrabble Irish immigrant past, and located only three blocks north of the house in which Mike Fiscus was raised. It long had been Mike's primary hangout, his father's in years before that, and one that Joseph remembered well from the times he hung with Fiscus there.

We were certain we'd find him. We'd just saunter in, pick him out, then sit down silently on either side. Mebbe flick an ash in his drink.

Heh.

Surprisingly, the bartender hadn't seen him for a while. "Try The Pub. He lives upstairs."

The Pub is on State Street, seven blocks between the State Capitol and the University of Wisconsin, with The Pub pushing close to the UW end. The street is closed to most motor vehicles, a predominantly pedestrian mall made up of gift, clothing and coffee shops, restaurants and bars. It also is the center of fun and frolic for the UW's approximately 40,000 students, three-quarters of them undergrads, and regiments of high-school kids and townies.

It was early in the evening, prime party night of the weekend, and the kids who had just arrived in town for the school year that would begin a week or so later were coming out on parade: scores of them, hundreds, a good many coeds who in the style of our age were done up to the nines in halter tops, shorts and mini-skirts, high strappy heels. Joseph and I did our best not to leer, though struggling and wracked with temptation.

Above The Pub was a notorious place. A couple floors of rooms for rent, one large bathroom and shower per floor. It was the home for years, coming and going, for some of the most unforgettable and often disreputable characters who ever could hustle up 50 bucks a week for the privilege to squat. It was something like living in the same sort of...quarters...you might find in, say, Tijuana, Mexico, if you were a young sailor on liberty, hungry for puss, who'd been driven up into the hills by a cabbie who chose to simply take his fare and drop you off rather than slitting your throat for your shoes. I had known folks off and on over the years who were Pubsters. On a scale of things, I've had many friends who tilt toward the peculiar.

It wasn't crowded yet as Joseph and I walked into the bar, maybe a half-dozen crows on the rail. Among them I expected to see Mike. One guy near us, I thought, might be him. I nudged Joseph. "There he is."

Joseph took a gander. "Naah, that's not him. That guy's too fat."

I checked again. It was true; I can't imagine Mike Fiscus blown up like a toad. We looked around some more. Finally, I asked a bartender. "Hey, you know Mike Fiscus? Has he been in lately?"

He got a sort of sour look on his face. "Mike's in the hospital. They came to get him Tuesday night."

The two old road warriors exchanged glances. It wasn't so much an expression of shock, even sadness, but more along the lines of a tired familiarity. We'd been here before.

We shuffled out, walked a half block to the little concrete park at the corner of Frances and State and slouched against the wall of a bordering boutique. Before us, the parade was heating up. The girls went by in twos, threes and fours, gibbering happily and laughing. We watched for a while, a couple grizzled old phuques in riding leathers and earrings, skulking about.

"C'mon," I said. "Let's get out of here before we're arrested."

Riding to Moonie's in New Glarus, 27 miles south, we were welcomed warmly and treated to another guest—a Marine buddy of Moonie's from central upstate. The two of them would get together a couple of times a year, mostly to remind each other, close as I can tell, that they are jarheads. They were in the backyard, both of them loaded and acting like boots who had just been let out of camp for a night. They hooted and hollered, laughed like hyenas, wrestled like bears, and at 4 a.m. in a bucolic rural valley otherwise still, their boisterous bellows and *esprit de curses* could be heard all the way to Belleville and Monticello.

It was cool, even chill, the grass wet with early morning dew, and Joseph and I sat away from the maddened lance corporals, mostly silent, huddled in our leathers and cloaks, closed in our thoughts.

Next morning, I found the hospital where Fiscus had been taken. I called his room. The answer, no real surprise here, was by a guy named Gary, one of Mike's long-time friends and a fella I'd known since grade school. Another old pal, Red, was there, too. I asked about Mike, explaining briefly the circumstances of our mission.

"It's too late, Fred," said Gary. "He's almost gone. He's so doped up he'd never know you were here.

"It's cancer."

Joseph thought we should go anyway, pay our respects. "We've come all the way down here," he said. "We ought to stop by."

I flashed briefly on the two of us, strong-arming the staff, guns blazing, storming our way in. The cavalry arrives.

"No, I don't think so."

Not under these circumstances.

I'd done it before, for my Roadhouse buddy, Bugs, when I'd gone to Alabama and got there a day or two before he died. Zonked to the gills on morphine, he had no idea I'd come.

We left for home late that morning, riding in the rain most of the way, coming up the Mississippi between the bluffs, crossing at Prescott and into the Cities.

Mike died a day later.

As time passed, I'd gotten to thinking about it—a fantasy, one Mike might have liked. I've imagined how it might have been had we gone there.

Mike is lying in bed, tubes sticking out, sucking air under an oxygen tent. His eyes flicker, the coma lifts briefly, and he awakens, gazing hazily about the room.

"This might be it," he is thinking. "End of the Trail.

"Hmm. Not quite as I'd imagined, but better than expected.

"Joseph and Freddie are here."

25

HARD RIDE TO DEADWOOD

The Black Hills

2011

Fred and Barbi at the Crazy Horse Memorial in the Black Hills.

26

Plan Ahead

I was 67 when I made the Boulder Run and 10 months later, we decided to ride to the Black Hills.

We are Barbi and I.

We'd been riding together for 10 years, me in the saddle, Barbi on the pillion. Although one year she logged some 5,000 to 7,000 miles back there, in recent years it was less. Most of our rides were of the 150- to 300-mile variety, which Barbi considers just fine, out and back home in a day. At other times, we'd stay over somewhere for one or two nights.

Truth be told, whereas I've ridden yer obligatory 100,000 miles in my life, modest in itself, the preponderance were rides of approximately the same length. On occasions, I'd turn 600, 700, even 900 miles over 24 to 36 hours, but not all that much. On the Shadows, especially, geared more for mid-range cruising, 300 miles is a purty full day, especially if you're the passenger, riding the uniformly narrow and under-padded pillion seat.

But once the Valk came along, all that had to change. The Valk, with barely 17,500 original miles on the OD when we bought it, was made for touring. And at 68 years old, like it or not, I was starting to push the OD.

The Black Hills for me, as for so many others, have always been of great allure. For one, there's the fact that it's pretty much the only thing close to real mountains in the entire Midwest. Technically, they're only high hills, the tallest with an elevation of slightly more than 7,000 feet, until you get to Wyoming or Colorado. It's a geological anomaly, a sort of shirttail cousin of the Rockies, distanced from the homestead by some seismic hop or other and plopped down smack in the middle of the Great Plains. Otherwise, for the Plains, most part anyway, the rest might as well be Iowa. Or Nebraska. Or western Minnesota. The rest of South Dakota, far as that goes.

Hand in hand with this geological curiosity—a volcanic outgrowth of the Tertiary Period, some 65 million to 2.5 million years old and rising up in all its grandeur, is an even deeper cultural mystique. The Hills, inhabited by Native Americans for centuries, stood for the period of roughly 100 years as the tribal homeland, and a sacred place, of the Lakota Sioux Nation.

This is a curious situation. Whereas the western Sioux had lived on the plains surrounding the Hills since the late 1700's, a time when they fought the Cheyenne and finally pushed them out of the country and into the southern Plains, the rest of the tribe had settled into central and eastern South Dakota and along the Minnesota River Valley, south and west of today's Twin Cities. The Hills, therefore, were a part of their land, but only after centuries of other occupations. Numbers of native peoples had lived there dating all the way back to 7,000 B.C., and in more recent times it had been home at various times to the Arikara, Crow, Pawnee, Kiowa and the late coming Cheyenne.

Indeed, however, it was the western Sioux—the Oglala, Hunkpapa, Minneconjou and Sans Arc tribes—who were there when the white man came. Their struggle to hold onto it was essentially resolved, and lost, over the next nine years, 1868-1877—from Red Cloud's War to Custer's Last Stand, a short war of retribution and revenge impelled by the U.S. government and quick return to the reservations, finally culminating in its bloodiness 13 years later at Wounded Knee.

The other appeal, modern times, is that the Black Hills is a motorcyclist's paradise. It's only 100 by 50 miles in area, a good deal of that virtually impassible unless you're riding an off-road bike or a four-wheeled rec vehicle, but of that which is accessible, it's right up there with the Rockies, southwestern deserts, Pacific Coast or mountain ranges of east Tennessee and North Carolina as among the most picturesque in the country.

This is celebrated of course by the Sturgis rally, an annual rendezvous of enormity that began quite inconspicuously in 1938 with a local club hosting and nine racers scrambling around a short track in the dirt, and since that time has grown to a week-long celebration involving as many as 400,000 to a half-million leather-clad pilgrims.

I've never been to the rally. I rode through Sturgis coming home from The Boulder Run, stopped for gas at the foot of the steep slope declining from Deadwood, where I'd spent a night, but never so much as dallied. I might have, but I was in a hurry that day. Moreover, whereas I've been to plenty of biker rallies in Wisconsin and Minnesota, I actually have an aversion to crowds—especially if they are huge—and especially if they include, as they invariably do, every sort of poseur, outlaw, bare-breasted-and-bottomed woman and drunken fool that the good Lawd ever created. Frequently, all on one street.

The congestion, noise and bravado, engines rumbling and howling, tires blowing apart in smoky burn-outs and stinking of smoldering rubber, rock-and-roll music blasted all day and most of the night, is interminable and annoying. Even at night and into the wee hours, bikers are compelled to continue riding through the streets and campgrounds, rolling on their throttles and rapping their pipes. There is little respite.

I have a saying, and you can call me a wimp or a pussy, I don't care: A little bit of a lot of bikers goes a long way. Fifty or a hundred or more, even less, are sure to stand out for their sheer presence and power in attitude, and all too commonly the wilder, more drunken or stupid among them who belch and fart and cuss and fight and tend to run into things.

On this trip, however, it would be only Barbi and me. Our way and the highway, the way I like it best.

We'd talked about it for several months, then in the weeks before we left I'd made sure the Valk was in fine fettle, checking tire wear, precious fluids, nuts and bolts, and having special telescopic "graduated" springs put in the front forks to prevent them from "damping" or diving so much in the front end when the hulk is slowed down or brought to a sudden stop. Without the fork upgrade, given the Valk's design, the heavy weight of the 92.7 cubic inch engine combined with a full fuel tank of nearly seven gallons, can lean toward the problematic with all that weight shifting forward, a handful to handle.

The last week or two before departure was devoted in great part to packing. Whereas the Valk Interstate has a tremendous capacity for luggage—20 pounds between the hard bags and trunk—there is a limit. The trunk will accommodate two helmets, but if that's where they're stashed, then we lose about a third of our total capacity. There are chrome racks on top of both bags and trunk, and for a long trip I will mount a T-bag on the trunk, then a roll bag on top of that. The hard bags are for storing tools, small repair parts and the rest of the doodads one persists in carting along—a lot of them which never will be used, but God hep ya if'n you happen to be out there some time, you need them but left them at home.

The T-bag, at some 20 inches in height, 13 inches wide and 9½ inches deep, is made of water-shedding fabric and holds a lot of stuff—in my packing, mostly, a week's worth of clothes. There also are four decent-sized pockets, two on each side, and a couple of others for maps. The roll bag is for things you need to get to fast—rain gear, water resistant gloves, rubber rain weegees which fit over your thumb so you can swipe the water from your visor, helmet screen defogger and the like. Below the trunk, I hung a rolled rubber poncho, Swiss Army type, which in a pinch can be fastened to the windshield, handlebars and the T-bag with metal clips and spread out from the side of the bike as a lean-to for temporary shelter.

But in all of this, there was a hitch: Barbi doesn't like wearing a helmet. I don't either, far as that goes, but as mentioned, whether wearing one or not, it's always nice to have it around. I can live with them. For this run, as on the trip to Boulder, I decided to wear it all of the time, at least on the major highways. Barbi was of another opinion.

"I'll wear it if it rains," she said. "Or if it gets windy or cold."

Although she's owned three over the years, Barbi has never found one that she likes. They're too heavy, she says, weighing on her neck, and too tight, scrunching her ears and pressing the sides of her head. They mess with her hair. These are the usual complaints people have about helmets, but Barbi takes them personally.

"Well, I'm going to wear mine," I said. "Where will we put yours?"

It would be easy enough to take up half the trunk, as I've said, but in terms of total load not economical. Besides, half of the trunk is where I'd decided to carry a fuel can to avoid the kind of situation I'd faced the year before, perilously close to running out of gas on a Sioux reservation.

I tried slinging both helmets with bungees at different places on the sides of the bike and the T-bag. Wherever I put them, I couldn't see out of at least one of my mirrors. Had I slung them on top of the roll bag, that atop the T-bag, it could have doubled as a sail. In South Dakota, where the winds blow heavy on the main line, a sail I didn't need.

It wasn't working, too little space for this and that, so I acquiesced.

Now, it's important to note here, should you not have figured it out already, this is not a "how-to" book, nor is it about practicality, common sense or safety. It's about things I've done on motorcycles, some of them silly and a few that run to stupid. This was one of the more stupid, so I therefore entreat all readers to take this into consideration—past, present and forward—and consider the source.

I put her helmet in one half of the trunk and left the fuel can behind. I did so reluctantly, granted, but that's the way it came down.

Fool me once, fool me twice—especially of my own volition—and I am the fool. Sometimes, I play the part purty well.

27

Rain on the Plain

It was early on a morning in late June, skies overcast, when we pulled out of the driveway from our home in the western 'burbs of the Twin Cities. Fifteen minutes later, turning south on State 169, it started to drizzle. There was construction ahead, and maybe an accident, so traffic was backed up, slowed to a crawl. The rain began to fall harder.

Splat. Splat, splat.

I turned to Barbi.

"Want to put on the helmet?" I asked.

She did.

I pulled over to the side and hauled it out. It wasn't raining hard enough to put on the rain gear. Under the circumstances, the helmet would suffice. She wore it all the way to the Black Hills, took it off there, as I did mine (wind in the hair, ya know?), and then we wore them again all the way from Deadwood back to Minnesota.

The first day's ride, save for intermittent drizzle, was uneventful. We made it to Sioux Falls, dashed on through and quartered for the night in Mitchell. It's not all that big, so we had time to buzz by the Corn Palace, which proved not so magnificent sitting there in the middle of a block as one might otherwise surmise from the postcards.

In the morning, moments after finishing our continental breffus, it started to rain—no drizzle, real rain. We loaded back up, donned our rain gear and set on our way. It rained all the way to Deadwood, 300 miles.

We were traveling I-90, if not the most scenic, the easiest route. Our first stop was at Chamberlain, the Missouri River, where we stretched among other sojourners, a dozen of them bikers, took a pee and a walk along the bluff and admired the majesty of the river below.

Next stop was for lunch, a place called Murdo, which caught my eye because of its main tourist attraction, an Old West Town reconstructed along the lines of 1880. It cost money to get in, the rain had let up but still was sprinkling, and I needed to make Deadwood by dark. We skipped the show and opted for lunch. There was a short string of railroad cars parked outside the fenced Old West Town, circa '50s or so, and a sign denoting a restaurant inside. We walked in, welcomed warmly by the ladies of the staff, and had ham and cheese sandwiches in one of the dining cars while we looked out the window at Old West Town cowpokes, guns hanging low over chaps, as they shuffled through the mud on the way to the next performance.

Leaving, we walked down a wooden, rain-slickened ramp. I was ahead, heard an eek! behind me, followed closely by a thump, and when I turned around, there was Barbi, sprawled on her arse. Another customer got to her before I did to help pick her up, and after a moment or two of examination, confirmed by her self-diagnosis, discerned that she was all right. A twisted knee, sore, but thankfully not seriously damaged. Which for me, if not for Barbi, was easy to say.

One thing overwhelmingly evident in South Dakota is how broad it is. It's not so much the actual width, mileage, although lengthy enough, but in the physical breadth of the place; the big sky, the "low rolling flatness," sheer immensity and understated majesty of it all. You can't help but think of the people who crossed it in the nineteenth century, the settlers moving west, in wagons and carts, on horseback and walking. What could they manage, fifteen miles a day? And if they weren't stopping in Wyoming or Montana, if they were moving on to

Utah or Oregon, say, it was going to be a journey that would last four to six months. Amazing.

So, here we are, zipping along at 75, which according to tipsters you can do all day out there on the interstate, but don't go any faster. That's where the highway patrol comes in. I'm told they're very strict.

As the afternoon went on, we found ourselves following a huge dark spot in the sky. By following, I mean the spot was out there ahead, taking up a good third of the horizon, and at each place the road turned, which doesn't happen that often, so did the spot. A very deep blue and purple, shading toward black, with flashing forked and double lightning bolts at all-too-regular intervals.

Then the rain came again—hard this time, harder than we'd run into all day.

I often run with my visor up, pushed back above the helmet to let in more air, which helps reduce interior condensation when it's humid and damp. Left up, however, if the rain comes down harder, ripples of it flow down the forehead mold and into your eyes. Now, I pulled it down nearly tight, leaving a small slit open at the chin piece to help cut the fogging. Visibility was getting tricky.

Before long, it was so tricky that I couldn't see—not much, anyway.

Periodically during the riding season, I put a solution on the outside of my visor to help water bead and disperse, same as I do on my windshield, but there comes a point in a hard-driving storm when that isn't sufficient anymore. This was fast becoming one of those. I started looking for someplace to bug out, an exit ramp with a service station, a side road with an abandoned steel shed, maybe even a large roadside kill, a fallen bison which I could eviscerate with my Leatherman so we could crawl into the protective womb and wrap the hide over us. Most optimistically, a wayside or overpass.

Another thing about South Dakota—there are no overpasses, very few anyway, because essentially there's nothing to pass over. Looking out from east-west I-90, personally speaking, I got to wondering how anyone ever gets north and south. But just as I was entertaining the dubious notion of just stopping, pulling over to the shoulder at risk of getting slammed by a semi, there it loomed midst the wash up ahead.

An overpass.

By Gawd, an overpass!

Hallelujah, Martha! Will ya look at that!

Slowing down, taxiing in, I saw that we'd been preceded. There was a cluster of bikes pulled off to the side, a narrow strip passing for a shoulder and set close to the concrete abutment. The riders were huddled about, one of them stepping out and waving, guiding us in. Their bikes lined up end to end, we got half of the Valk underneath, then climbed off and joined them.

It was five couples from Indiana, all riding Harleys, who'd come from Sioux Falls that morning. Nobody introduced anyone else; we just all shared the dilemma, hung around joking, waiting it out. It was probably 20 minutes, then everyone mounted up and pulled away, one by one, with a flourish and spray.

Not far down the road, we came upon Wall. Everybody anywhere near it, of course, who hasn't already been there, has to stop. It's the home of Wall Drug, world-famous for being...Wall Drug. A tourist mecca, the "most popular destination in America" as hailed, it spreads out over two blocks on the main drag in a series of connected Western-style shops, and across the street is an open-faced saloon, a large one. A sophisticated flea market in certain respects, Wall Drug displays everything from practical goods to trinkets to paintings to carvings to T-shirts, hats and boots, ice cream and free water to boot.

We were there barely half an hour, during which time the sun actually came out, first time that day. With that, however, it didn't stop raining, so we hung out with the masses under the overhang, drinking coffee and free water and enjoying the splash. Of sunshine, that is. Fittingly, for all the happy campers, there was a rainbow.

Wall is the gateway to the Hills, a harbinger of promise for those heading west. When you reach Wall, the Hills are not far beyond. Or so it seemed, anyway, as we hustled out.

We could see the Hills ahead, the outline at first, then the sense they are mountains. Big hills, anyway, very big hills. We also got the sense after a long day, we were closing on our destination, which for Barbi, a real trouper to this point, no whining, no pleading, bucking right up, was also approaching a sense of urgency. She was tired, she was sore, she was wet. So was I, but having looked at my map, nearing Rapid City, I knew we still had more than 50 miles to go. It was getting close to six o'clock.

"Shouldn't we be there by now?" Barbi asked.

"Um, no—pretty soon. Maybe another hour or so."

"Why should it take an hour? We've passed signs for Sturgis for miles."

"Wahl, from Sturgis to Deadwood it's still up the mountain a ways. It's still gonna take a while."

On a bright and sunny June morning, it would be a real treat. A very pretty ride. On a rainy evening, turning chilly with fog hanging low in the Hills, it was a last tired climb. After a bit of confusion in Sturgis, during which Barbi questioned my navigation and I yelled and threw a map across a parking lot. I recognized the route, once I got on it, having come down it the summer before. I knew we were close.

"The sign said nine miles," said Barbi as we climbed the mountain through drizzle and fog. "Are you sure you know where you're going?"

Ha! Yes I do, thought I, and as we popped over one more rise and eased down through a curving left-hander sliding into the gulch, there it was.

Deadwood.

28

Seth Bullock Slept Here

We stayed at the Bullock Hotel. After watching the HBO TV series "Deadwood," the best scripted and seemingly authentic Western drama of its kind I've ever seen, how could we not

Seth Bullock, the hero, was the first sheriff of Deadwood, helped tame the town, later expanded his hardware store interests, became a true city father, lived to a ripe old age and went down in history as probably the second-most famous historical figure to ever come out of there behind James Butler Hickok, whose overriding claim to fame was getting shot in the back of the head during a poker game at Saloon No. 10. Or maybe Bullock was the third-most famous, behind Calamity Jane. They're all buried there.

In 1894, his warehouse surviving a devastating town fire, Bullock and his partner, Sol Star, built the hotel on the site. Restored and renovated a couple of times in the twentieth century, it's still there, resplendent in a vaguely tired but clean sort of way to emulate what it was like way back when. In that sense, we found it germane.

Bullock's ghost is reputed to haunt the place, although it did not cross our paths. I'm not very good at ghosts, anyway, having also spent a night at the supposedly spooked Grand Hotel in Jerome, Arizona, a former hospital where injured miners died horrible, screaming deaths, without encountering any myself, nor did I on this occasion.

I will admit to having the eerie feeling that I once shared my apartment with one in a house in which I lived in Madison many years previous, but we never met formally.

There's a casino on the main floor and a restaurant, but in my opinion, the liveliest spot at the Bullock is a basement bar called Bully's, and though lively is not how I normally would characterize a small low-lit room with four customers and a bartender, it was the latter who helped bring it to life.

Justin Hogen is his name, and he's usually there two nights a week. He is not loquacious, but if you sound him out, he's a storehouse of local legend and lore, stories delivered with a wry sense of humor and timing. He was among the highlights of our whole trip.

Another of these, tamer than most, was Woody's Wild West Old Time Photos, just a few doors down from the hotel. We wandered in there the second afternoon of our stay. You can find these places all over—the Wisconsin Dells, for example, 50 miles north of Madison—and although always intrigued, I'd never seized the initiative to stop in and go through with the clicks.

For a Wild West photo, Deadwood seemed the ideal place to start, so I hustled Barbi over there and we quickly decided on a setting, a Western barroom, natch, and she went upstairs to the dressing rooms to pick out some frills. I had no problem; I was going to wear what I had on. All I needed was a hat and gun. I tried on several hats, found one that fit—sort of a Butch Cassidy model—and asked the assistant what she might have in the way of guns.

"Colt? Remington? Patterson? Anything like that?

She wasn't that familiar with them, she said, but she'd see what she could rustle up. She went through a box in a back room and reappeared with a faux pearl-handled, silver-plated revolver.

"1851 Navy Colt, .36 caliber, same pistol that Wild Bill used to favor. Poifect," I said, and slipped it into my belt.

(Wahl, okay, I had one of my own—the .357 worn cross-draw under my vest, but as liberal as South Dakota's gun laws may be, I thought it imprudent to whip out the Smith and brandish it about on the main drag of Deadwood. It remained in its holster.)

Barbi came down, done up fetchingly—queen of the dance hall girls—and hopped up on the bar. I put a boot on a wooden crate, leaned back and stood next to her. Five shots, slow and deliberate, and we got shot good.

Our rides through the Hills were splendid. No rain, sunshine and reasonably cool for that time of year. With the Sturgis rally still weeks down the road, we damn near had the place to ourselves. Staying in Deadwood, we were fairly removed from the other centers of action. We did your standard *tourista* stuff—Mount Rushmore, the Crazy Horse Monument, a spin through Custer State Park where the burros and buffalo roam, and in my mind the high point, a ride through the Needles, 14 miles of narrow, twisting State Highway 87, much of it up-and-down hairpin turns.

It's so narrow in places that vehicles have to stop and wait while one or more pass by them coming the other way. This is especially true of a series of tunnels, blasted through the granite rock, at least one of which is only nine feet wide. After that, I figure I can take the Valk through damn near anything short of a flooded creek or mud hole. Great for my confidence, and Barbi's as well.

Having never ridden this far, Barbi was holding up nicely. She'd been through the rough weather with nary so much as a sniffle.

Now, however, on our last night in the Hills, we were about to be tested again.

29

Oasis

By the next morning the weather, which had been turning warmer, took a turn to the hot. Packing the bike, I was sweating. Night before, I had asked Justin the bartender what the best road back to Minnesota might be.

"All of the roads in South Dakota suck," he answered authoritatively.

I chose what I thought to be the lesser of the evils I had previously traveled—State 34, which becomes U.S. 14. I'd done U.S. 212 and I-90, so this time I'd try running between, the road to Pierre.

For the first leg, everything proceeded nicely. In preparation for the heat, I'd purchased a couple of large canvas bandanas made with slits in the center and pockets in which you can stuff a half package of ice. In extreme heat, the ice will melt over 70, 80 miles, but in the process provide a profound cooling effect. We wore them backwards, pockets down our backs, and without them, I think, we well might have perished. We also were wearing our helmets, which if nothing else kept our brains from broiling like eggs. So insulated, we rolled along merrily, classical music blasting loud from the stereo.

The heat index was 95. Next day, it was 105.

First stop for a refill of ice was White Owl, as much as we could see a lone feed and gas station, nearly nothing else around. I checked the gas tank, still seemed to have plenty left for the next fill, so I didn't bother to put any in. Instead, we just loaded up on bottled water and foo-foo juice, rehydration solutions.

Today, this hearkens in my experiences back to Eagle Butte, the year before, when I passed on gas in the naïve expectation of finding it somewhere else up the road at such time that I conveniently needed it. Ha!

Less than a mile out of White Owl, we passed a sign: "Last service for 74 miles."

Hmm. If they were telling us that from here for the next 74, we were on our own, why didn't the dipshits put up the sign before White Owl instead of after it? And if I weren't such a nimrod, why didn't I have that spare fuel can in my trunk?

I should have just turned around. Feeling dense, however, and trusting greatly in the enormous seven-gallon capacity in the tank of the Valk, I blundered on.

If you live in the Midwest, they say, there are two seasons to a year: winter and roadwork. This proved true once again as we rode toward Pierre. A highway crew was at work, at that stage in the midst of laying down gravel for a stretch of the next 14 miles. We were delayed. There was only one lane in service, so traffic going our way had to wait 20 minutes for that from the other. A woman in a hardhat and highway department vest, brandishing a stop sign, brought us to halt.

It was around 2 p.m., I'd say, and the sun was high. There was no breeze. No trees. No shade. We were first in line, a UPS van and a fuel tanker behind us. I shut down the bike and we got off.

I was taking a Zen-like approach. Just roll with it, such as it may be, don't seize up with the moment, let it pass. Barbi, I saw, was closer to a seizure, nigh high to a faint. We'd left our helmets on—under that sun, the broiled egg antidote. Between heavy perspiration and the dribbles of melting ice from the bandanas, our light cotton shirts were stained brown and red. It was nearly like sitting in a sauna. High above, a buzzard circled.

I made the buzzard part up.

But for the rest of it, had we stayed there another hour, I'm certain that years from now when archeologists mined the trail uncovering cattle skulls, pottery shards and arrowheads, they'd eventually come upon the bleached bones of two intrepid but foolhardy travelers, a man and a woman, approximate age in the 60's, their death's head grins beaming out ghoulishly from cracked, weathered helmets, marking indelibly for both science and posterity the timeless dark humor of their ironic demise.

In the nick of time, we got the green flag. A department car came along, a line of traffic behind it, and the driver, another woman, made a U-turn and signaled us on. Fourteen miles through the gravel and dust, 40 mph max. For my part, I was glad the gravel was passable.

It was some time after that, surmounting a seemingly endless column of hills, each one offering a brief glimpse of the surrounding vastness before dropping again into the following dip, that I began checking my gas gauge. It was getting down there. A few miles later, cresting yet another of these mounds, I sensed a sputter, a cough and a fart. I reached down to my left, flicked the fuel switch from "Run" to "Reserve" and heard Barbi ask, "Are we running out of gas?"

What? What?

Naah. No such chance.

I was calculating in my head. How many miles left to Pierre, how much gas in the tank? How much to slow down to conserve what I had? Worst part of all, how to explain it to Barbi if indeed we ran out? How to face the recrimination, the humiliation of it all, the fact that here we were in the middle of Bumphuque, melting into the plain, all because I was a doofus.

I tried to rationalize, a lame attempt to convince me it was Barb's fault. She's the one who didn't want to wear her helmet, squandering space in the trunk for the first 15 miles of our 600-mile trip and displacing a 1.25-gallon can. Our life's blood. That, and our foo-foo juice.

I nursed the Valk's descent into the Missouri River valley, another long grade, I coasted most of the way. We filled up, hungrily at the first place we could, two pumps for truckers, credit card only, at west edge of the city. I had dodged another small bullet, not in the least Barbi's wrath.

It was 4 p.m., the sun was glaring, when we crossed the bridge in Pierre and pulled over at the first pub I found. Pub is not exactly the right word for it; rather, a bar and grill of the kind where the only thing missing was a bowling alley attached. We slugged down a couple glasses of ice water, nursed a couple of beers (Grain Belt Premium, a Minnesota staple, light and leaning toward flavorless, but with a slight sweet spot at the swallow that redeems all the rest). Barbi solicited ice.

We studied our map, conversed over packing it in somewhere around there or moving on, and decided to give moving a shot. Fifty miles east was Miller, population 1,323, a place Barbi had heard about from a biker at work who has stayed there off and on during his annual rides to Sturgis.

The first motel in Miller was full. So was the second, the Dew Drop Inn Motel, straight across U.S.14. Seems that the powers that be swung four major construction projects in the area, and whereas normally there would be vacancies, now they'd been booked solid for the previous three months. I sat out on the bike while Barbi sweet-talked the owner. He called six bed-and-breakfast spots, and on the last one, we scored. It was only three blocks away, and Gawd, what a welcome surprise.

I was ready to crash in a crack pad, but this was the Dakota House, five rental rooms in a large old Victorian-style home, sprawled on a tree-shaded corner on Broadway, the main drag, and family-owned and operated for decades. There was a broad railed porch with pillowed wicker chairs and a couch around three-quarters of the house and a veranda. There was even a faint breeze starting to blow from the southeast.

Our room and the bathroom were immaculate, the bed soft and the shower working. On a tip from the owner, we walked two blocks to the Turtle Creek Saloon and had ribeyes, the trimmin's and tall, frosty steins of beer. I sat on the porch for a while after we got back. The breeze was cooling, the moon shining overhead. A calm, quiet night, most reviving for me, in one of those very special places in America, towns where nobody yet locks their door.

Hot and humid again by mid-morning, we repacked our gear and lit out on the last leg of the trip. I won't belabor, only that we hightailed it through Huron, then on to Brookings for lunch. We zoomed off again, and now, like most of us who feel that homing hum deep down inside as we draw near, I finally begin to relax.

Oh, yeah, I know. Riding a motorcycle is supposed to be a relaxant, or could be, but with things going to hell in a basket and all of us with it, riding has turned into a challenge. Every time you go out there.

I met a guy once in Wisconsin, a former member of a biker gang in central Minnesota who had fled there for reasons of health (two 9mm rounds in his belly), to live rurally and to find peace on earth. He said one of his greater pleasures used to be coming home from work at 5, getting on the bike and going out for an hour-or-two leisurely scoot.

"You can't do that anymore," he said. "It's like an X-sport out there."

A day after we got home, the shit hit the fan. From Marshall to Montevideo to Willmar and Litchfield, 60-80 mph straight winds slashed through southwest Minnesota, the same country we'd traveled just 24 hours before.

That day the temperature in the Twin Cities reached 107. The heat index was 120.

Reflecting on the whole thing, Barbi asked if I could pick just one highlight from the whole trip, what it would be.

"Making it out there and back," I said.

30

MALADIES

Here, There and Around

1980–Present

Lt. Col. McFred, 1st Hamel Motorized Cavalry, at the outset of a run beginning at Inn Kahoots in Hamel.

31

The Dupe's

Admittedly, I am showing signs of running down.

Breaking down, to be more precise.

It's not a matter of energy lost; gratefully, I still retain much of that which I've always held, which remains adequate. A 450-mile ride on the Valk, comfortable as it is with the Ultimate seat, leaves me at dismount with no real fatigue, aches or pains.

Rather, it is a growing compendium of pieces unraveling—hip, groin, hands and eyes—starting to wear out. The ravages of age, as they say.

The hip, in which bursitis has set, so far is no big deal. I feel it when I'm lifting heavy things or pushing them around, but on the bikes it manifests only rarely as a sort of "catch" in my joint. To relieve it, I'll either put the leg out onto the highway peg or if traffic is light, stand up on my footpegs and ride a few feet like that.

The groin problem, a hernia on the right side, hasn't meant too much, either. I've decided to let it be until such time it begins to swell unduly or pain. I've been told that surgery for hernias is not always successful. It can leave you hurting, the scar tissue resistant to heal thoroughly so that the semi-closed wound continues weeping. Sometimes folks have to go back to have the docs cut them again. Sometimes the hernia comes back.

It is my hands, really, historically, that have been the source of my greatest concern over whatever annoyances arise that may negatively affect my ability to ride a motorcycle.

I have a condition. Dupuytren's contracture it's called, and the upshot is the growth of hard, cartilage-like tissue in the palms and in and around the sheaths in one's fingers through which the tendons pass. The growth (unchecked and invasive. like tumors, but benign) impedes upon the tendons, precluding them from sliding back and forth, the fingers losing their flexibility. What you are left with, sooner or later if left untreated, are as many as the last three digits on either hand beginning to contract, and then slowly keep drawing back, claw-like at the extreme, toward the palm.

In the bad old days, the fingers bent back enough, perhaps even to the point of nails growing into the palm, somebody would eventually have to come along and lop 'em off. Mebbe even the guy with the fingers.

Worse yet, depending on yer point of view, it can show up in your feet or even your pee-pee, your schwanz, for that matter.

Imagine.

I can but don't want to.

Identified medically in 1831 by Baron Guillaume Dupuytren, a French anatomist and military surgeon known otherwise for having treated Napoleon's hemorrhoids, the condition, widely defined as genetic, has been around a long time. Curiously, it is known primarily among men of Scandinavian and northern European descent and statistically speaking hardly anyone else. There are vestiges among men in the Mediterranean and Japan, but seldom if ever in women, blacks, or peoples of any other ethnicity or region.

Curiously, it became known at some point as the "Viking Disease" because in its earliest appearance it was found predominantly among Norsemen and those of their descent.

I've speculated about this. There is a side theory to causation of the Dupe's, as I call it, which says the condition can be triggered and accelerated by trauma. What did the Norsemen do for centuries? Row. Row, row, row. Row their arses off in their long boats as they raged for centuries across Northern Europe and the British Isles. That, and swinging heavy swords and battle axes.

Another group with a high incidence is Scots, particularly true of bagpipers. You move those digits repetitively for part of a lifetime and you start to get a small and ring finger that aren't working like you're used to, you're washed up. Might as well march, tootling away however off key, straight off into the North Sea.

Otherwise, far as theories go, other possible contributors if not causes may be diabetes, epilepsy, liver disease, alcoholism or smoking.

Wahl, I smoke. It's my only remaining vice. Otherwise, there's only one factor besides genetics that may possibly apply to nudging along my condition.

I spent some 30 years traumatizing my hands. Or mauling them, more precisely.

Wrestling in high school and a year in college, I can't say hurt all that much. One year, because of sprained thumbs, I wrestled several matches with both taped to the sides of my hands. Inconvenient, but not the kind of thing that ought to become congenital.

It was softball, by my take, which may have triggered the fingers. Fast-pitch was the game, where the softball ain't soft, nor as large and mushy as you find in slow-pitch, a grandly popular sandlot game. The softball in fast-pitch is smallish and hard, slightly larger than a baseball, and as a catcher, which is the position I played, over the course of 15 years I caught the ball in a mitt hundreds of thousands of times. Most every time I caught one, it went smack. If I didn't catch it in the mitt (the web ideally but mostly in the pocket, right at the base of the fingers) I was just as likely to have it carom off my meat hand in the process of getting chipped with low pitches in the dirt or foul tips driven back off the bat. It was early on that I started taping all my fingers with adhesive.

In the Navy, when I played for the *Iwo Jima* for a spring and most of a summer when we were in dry dock at Puget Sound Naval Shipyard in Bremerton, Washington, we had games two or three times a week in a base league with a nifty little park, grandstands and lights. We had three pitchers who I called "Fast, Faster and the Fastest." After a game, I'd go back to the ship and up the ladder to sick bay to soak my hand in ice water–usually the left hand, which wore the mitt, but sometimes the right, the meat hand, on nights when the balls were taking especially cruel bounces.

After softball, resigning the sport not long after the night some 10 years later when while at bat with a 3-2 count and guarding the dish I took a fastball that broke up and in at the last split second and despite bailing out, hit me square in the nose. ("I'm not making enough money at this to come out here and let these nuts throw at my head," I said in my retirement speech.)

At that point, I turned to volleyball.

Not nearly so much an impact sport as softball, V-ball does however leave fingers and ankles vulnerable. As a setter, I got my hands on the ball plenty enough, often on most every volley, so following along in the course of my catcher days there were hundreds of thousands of additional times over the next 15 years that I tipped a ball in the air off my fingertips. Or misplayed it enough to cause a minor or major jam.

Maybe a combined 30 years of that sort of thing had no effect whatsoever. Maybe it was coincidence. Fact is, though, far as genetics goes, no one else in either my extended family or any ancestors as we know ever had Dupuytren's contracture. Only other one I know of in fact is my son, who at the age of 18 broke a hand while batting in a semi-pro baseball game, a fastball that hit on a knuckle and drove it so deep into his hand that it's never been seen again. In his late '20s, he developed a hard little knot in the palm and had it examined.

He was diagnosed with the Dupe's, an early onset, considering his age.

Go figger.

So, what's any of this have to do with motorcycles?

Only this:

I still hold strength in my hands—but at times in the past when the contractures have been most severe, I've had to go around on the bikes two-fingering the levers because as many as three or four fingers on either hand wouldn't straighten out well enough for me to wrap them over the top and grab a whole handful.

That's doable with the Shadow, given its lighter weight, but for the Valk—wahl, try feathering the brake lever with two fingers when you need to stop *now* while coming down from 75 miles per hour to zero on an elephantine 840-pound missile of aluminum, rubber, plastic and steel, and I mean *now*! Don't work so good.

What I've done to compensate is have surgeries. Until the past year, when an enzyme was finally made clinical that can be injected directly into a knot with the likely outcome of dissolving it in its whole, the only treatment for Dupuytren's was going under the knife. In that, they'd peel away the skin, dig around for a knot and start carving away at it with scalpels. The last one I had, it took an hour and 40 minutes and the doc went through 11 blades. I was under local anesthesia.

It's actually sort of neat. You can feel and hear them scraping, but you feel no pain. If anything, it's the tourniquet wound tightly around the upper bicep that after an hour or so brings you close to swearing or screaming. Gnashing yer teef, if you're a real guy.

Since '89, I've had 8 ½ surgeries. The Dupe's has a high rate of recidivism.

(The half came after they wheeled me into recovery one time and observed that the pinky on my right hand was turning purple. They'd snipped a vein, not knowing that another one had previously become broken or crushed through either the Dupe's or some previous surgical misstep. I wasn't getting any blood. Back to the OR, where they spliced it with a morsel of vein they cut from my wrist. Everything dandy.)

Of late, through the enzyme, there's been an improvement of treatment, so to speak. The needle is long, the enzyme expensive. There is no anesthesia (freezing the area, they reason, that they're less likely to fine-spot their real target). Over the matter of a few minutes they shoot the shit in.

Normally in these situations, like, say, going to the dentist, I try to get outside my body—just sort of finding someplace where I can float away and hold myself in abeyance for a few minutes until they've had their way. In my experience, this method has about a 50-50 chance of succeeding, so this time around I decided that instead I would "embrace the pain."

Wow! What a rush!

Hurt me! Hurt me! Yeah, that's it! Deeper! Give it another good push!

Jesusphuquingchristalmighty!

But okay, enough of that. That's the matter of my fingers and hands. I've dealt with it for a long time, I'll deal with it some more, at least until the bastids no longer will bend. For the time being, they're working again quite fine and sufficiently.

'Course, I'll never be able to play the piano, but then, I've never played it before. At least the hands are still working well enough to manage both the bikes and a computer keyboard.

Stuff of life.

32

Haze Near the End of the Tunnel

Next came the eyes.

I was on the way back from Michigan recently, a 450-mile ride, the final leg of a 1,000-mile cruise.

It started well enough, leaving Ada at 7:30 a.m. and catching the Lake Express Ferry to Milwaukee, leaving Muskegon at 10. The 2 ½-hour cruise covering 90 miles was smooth and not rocky, my Dramamine tablets proving unnecessary. Milwaukee to Madison went swiftly. I dithered about in Madison for a couple of hours, seeking to run down old friends, and eventually pulled out around 4:45. I rode the interstate to Black River Falls, about halfway from Madison to the Twin Cities, and pulled in at a truck stop for an iced coffee and gas.

Heading back out northwest, late afternoon, the sun had dropped itself in the worst possible place, low over the road and right in my eyes. It was like nothing I've ever seen before, cars and trucks and the horizon before me all shaded nearly one-dimensionally in a smoky haze of brown and gray. I couldn't see clearly much more than 30, 40 feet ahead. I held up my left hand in front of my eyes, holding the throttle at around 70 with my right, and struggling to see the lane lines.

Next thing I knew, there was an exit road off to the right, normally one I'd see coming a quarter-mile away. This one I missed. But in its place I found somewhere between—between the exit road and the highway, that is, a no-man's land of dirt and concrete and a drop-off, and I was headed right at it.

Instinctively, I ducked back to the left, into the right lane in which I'd been riding. There was no one there. Had there been, I would have been phuqued. Smashed. A semi, mebbe.

Splat. Like the bug on the windshield.

Thirty or so miles up the road, I pulled off at Osseo, decided to wait, let the sun go down. It did, and off again I started. At least it's dark, no more sun in my eyes. The last 130 miles into Minnie ought to be a snap.

Whoa, ho, ho. Not so fast there, old fella.

T'was a time when my vision was absolutely peachy, 20/15, which means I could see things at 20 feet that for other folks, they'd need 15.

It stayed that way for half of my life. Then, around the age of 40, things went to hell overnight.

I was reading the paper, fair light in mid-afternoon, and all of a sudden I saw these ants marching across the page. I tilted it back and forth, standard-size newsprint, and I could no longer see it so clearly.

T'was a time, shooting a rifle, when I could knock the nut off a gnat, metaphorically speaking, you unnerstan'.

Now I needed to have spectacles—then bifocals, then trifocals, fer Chrissake—and though as years have passed by I have adjusted reasonably well, I still find it inconvenient and nettling to be sighting a rifle at 100 yards, 50 or 25, and have to keep moving my head ever so slightly up and down to find the right lens to pinpoint the target.

Same is true of shooting a pistol, which God in his infinite mercy has helped to design so that anyone with an eye problem finds that the distance between the eyes through the arms and hands and to the front sight is—just plain not right for anyone with an eye problem. I manage just fine at 15-20 feet, which actually is "point shooting" and you really don't have to adjust much but to keep your eye on the front sight. Twenty-five feet becomes a problem.

Of late, matters worse, it's been determined that I have a cataract growing in my right eye.

It was diagnosed last spring during an exam when I was having my eyeglass prescription changed. The optometrist said the eye is working at only around 70 percent, and that sooner or later I'd need to have something done. For a few weeks following, I kept putting it off, hoping that I could get through the season without going under the knife again (or possibly a laser), having it removed.

If there were hints, it was during night driving. Things on the "outside of things" that were starting to become fuzzy, something that Barbi had noticed when I was driving the car.

Now, it was there in a hurry. All of a sudden. Totally.

Headlights and taillights were blurred, road signs I couldn't see or read until I was upon them. Worst of all, in my peripheral vision I could no longer distinguish roadside landmarks, things that I'd recognize intuitively after so many comings and goings, even in the dark. I could barely see the lane lines.

It was like riding in a tunnel—an alley–and riding nearly blind. It concluded with the last 50 miles through the beltlines of St. Paul and Minneapolis, the "Journey of Death," as we have referred. It was a trying experience.

The next day, safe at home by the good grace once more, I made an appointment to have it corrected. At this writing, I'm on the verge of that.

These things aside, what's left is my reactions. That, and anticipation, the ability to still sense and see things coming, make the right decision, get the hell past them or otherwise out of the way. This is most critical. Without it, no rider is safe on the road. And for any who may start to feel older and worn upon, those faculties dwindling, it's the most important signal to follow as to whether you keep riding or not.

Used to be I was naturally quick. Hell, today, most of the time, if I drop something from my hand I can still catch it before it hits the floor.

So far, so good. In the kitchen, anyway.

But on the road, it's a life or death story. No country for old men.

I once asked my father why old people look so crabby.

"There's a couple of reasons," he said. "The older you get, the more your muscles lose strength and tension. In your face, the muscles sag.

"And besides, it's not that much fun getting old."

Afterword

Spring came late this year, but not unexpectedly. Spring almost always comes late to Minnesota and in most average years, it's probably June before the rains and winds abate sufficiently for those of us not quite so hardy as others to finally fire it up and scoot about.

There were a few days in March, the false spring that fooled nobody but the young and inexperienced and perhaps several hundreds of thousands of out-of-state travelers who happened to be passing through. But then came a typical cool and splashy April and a following May in which we recorded the second highest rainfall for the month in state history.

Hence, we took it to June, sweltered of late through the hottest July on record, and now look forward to what we hope is an even break between here and the end of October.

I stored the Shadow in the garage over the winter, and the Valk stayed at Empire Cycle—my men in Loretto. My men are Adam and Eric, a couple young guys I happened across three, four years ago, who after training two years at the Honda school in Phoenix, decided to stick together and start their own business. They opened it in their garage, I stumbled upon them and became their first customer. They're well rounded, can fix damn near anything from a Harley panhead to an off-roader to a snowmobile, but for me they've been a particular godsend: They specialize in old Japanese bikes.

One thing that distinguishes me from what I consider the next level of biker is that I do very little of my own mechanics. Never have. Ain't my long suit. Oh, I can do some of yer average stuff, and in case of an emergency I always try to bring along a roll of duct tape. I put air in the tires, gas in the tanks, keep a close eye on the temperature and tachometer gauges, the oil light, and I may even twist this or that with a wrench or a screwdiver and occasionally cobble something together with a bit of glue, duct or electrical tape. I've managed to run out of gas only once.

But for anything very important I've long depended on a few good people who can do what I can't. Collectively over the years it's made a huge difference in the performance of the bikes and the confidence I have in riding them.

One nod goes to Joe Puccio, who was working at Madison Motor Sports when I first met him, then later opened a shop of his own, Motorcycle Solutions. Another nearby shop in Minnesota is Hamel Power, where Bobby O'Connor and his right-hand man Larry were great to me for several years, even though I was riding Hondas and their specialty is Harleys and customs. Turns out they took care of me mostly because my bikes are so clean; that, and because they decided early on in the process that whatever else I may be, I'm a purty good shit.

There are other folks I could mention, lots of them along the way, and in particular for the past 12 years, a dozen or so who've made me feel welcome in Minnesota. It's greatly appreciated. I was nobody when I arrived here, am still nobody now, but there's a nice group of friends and acquaintances who I've come to call the "1st Hamel Motorized Cavalry."

Thanks to all of you.

Mechanically lame, I compensate romantically, sometimes likening my bikes to horses.

This stems, I am sure, from an imaginative yearning that goes back to childhood: I wanted to be a man on a horse, a "cowboy" in the general vernacular, or simply a lone rider crisscrossing the Plains, roaming the frontier in the American West.

I suspect strongly that I'm not the only one who feels this way.

The rider needs a trusty steed. He feeds and waters, strokes and brushes, whispers and heals, gives it a name and they develop a relationship. You take care of the horse, the horse takes care of you.

Speaks for us all in a way.

The rest, the mental, psychological and physical parts, is largely up to me.

Most important are the reactions—do I still have them? Are they still equal to the tests of the road? Can I still keep my focus, be aware and anticipate? Do I still hold that edge?

I won't belabor. Let's just say that we all have some damn thing or other, crosses to bear, and the older you get the more likely they are to befall you.

On the whole, I consider myself fortunate to have had the opportunity to ride, to live, and come through it all as well as I have.

There are still a few rides left in me. Granted, the perils of the road have become far more intimidating, even more than that since I've written this book and taken the time to sit back, review it all and contemplate. I am more keenly aware of the risk factors now, the close calls I've personally experienced, than ever I admitted before writing it. Perhaps it is nearing time to retire.

But no, not quite yet.

One More Ride, mebbe a few more than that.

I still treasure my totem bag, still look to the skies off and on before heading out, pay my respects to whomever may be paying attention—the Great Spirit, I prefer to assume.

But I no longer look at it with any sense of bravado, no challenging war cry flung from the throat of a bold but foolhardy young bucko. Rather, it now is muted, offered humbly, sincerely and with reverence. A whispered prayer.

Hoka-hei!

It's a *good* day to die.

Fred Milverstedt
Plymouth, Minnesota
July 2012

About the Author

Fred Milverstedt was born and raised in Madison, Wisconsin, served three years in the U.S. Navy and graduated from UW-Madison in 1969. A former journalist, columnist and multitasking writer and editor, he has written of sports, politics, higher education, and popular culture. He is the co-founder of *Isthmus*, a Madison weekly now in its 37th year of publication. With his dear partner Barbi and two cats, he lives in Plymouth, Minnesota, where he shoots guns, roots for the Badgers and Packers and keeps an eminently fine flower garden.